The Christ of God

The

CHRIST OF GOD

by
Horatius Bonar

edited by
Kent W. Clark

'I believe that thou art the Christ, the Son of God.' – John 11:27

The Christ of God
by Horatius Bonar
edited by Kent Ward Clark

Printed in the United States of America

ISBN 9781613790496

Unless otherwise indicated, Bible quotations are taken from The King James Version.

www.xulonpress.com

'FOR IN HIM DWELLETH ALL THE FULLNESS OF THE GODHEAD BODILY' (Col 2:9).

'AND WE BELIEVE AND ARE SURE THAT THOU ART THAT CHRIST, THE SON OF THE LIVING GOD' (JOHN 6:69).

'AND THE WORD WAS MADE FLESH, AND DWELT AMOUNG US' (JOHN 1:14).

'BLESSED ARE THEY THAT HAVE NOT SEEN, AND YET HAVE BELIEVED' (JOHN 20:29).

'WHOSOEVER BELIEVETH THAT JESUS IS THE CHRIST IS BORN OF GOD' (1 JOHN 5:1).

DEDICATION

I wish to dedicate this book to the elect of God who gather in buildings with steeples but find no gospel food for their souls. I dedicate the reprinting of The Christ of God to those who cry out each Lord's day in their church tombs, "Sirs, we would see Jesus." May our Sovereign Lord be pleased to rend the heavens and make known through the pages of the book that Name that is above every NAME!

To the little child of God who struggles through the slough of life and has no assurance, may you find rest as you read the pages of The Christ of God.

To the lost sheep of God, may you see CHRIST THE PURPOSE of God and THE THOUGHT of God and THE CHRIST of God!

ACKNOWLEDGMENT

It has been my great desire for much of my 45 years of ministry to give myself to reprinting the books of great servants of God who are presently with the Lord, but while here on this earth exalted HIS NAME!

Although having much doubt as to my own gifts to write of His Grace and Mercy, I have set out to exalt that worthy name with pen.

Neither of these desires would see fruition without financial support to undertake the task. I cannot say thank you enough to Mr. Ray Holm and Mr. Scott Gillespie for your support in this endeavor. The two of you have made it possible to reprint The Christ of God. I am sure that the elect of God shall rejoice in the reading of its pages and that elect sinners yet uncovered, while reading, will find HIM to be their sustenance.

INTRODUCTION

In no way would I compare myself to the great man of God, Horatius Bonar, but I do know his Savior. In the beginning pages of this book you will find a message that I have preached all over the country — "What's His Name?" I have added it to these pages only that you might see the centrality of Jesus Christ. There is a name that shall endure forever. There is a name to which every knee shall bow and every tongue shall confess.

There is a name that Satan and his demons have attempted to wipe from the pages of history. It is that worthy Name of Jesus Christ.

May God cause you to stand to your feet, lift your hands toward heaven and say aloud, "Worthy is the lamb that was slain."

Amen.

PREFACE

I do not know that I can preface the following Chapters more suitably than by quoting the words of the Apostle John in his first Epistle:

That which was from the beginning,
Which we have heard,
Which we have seen with our eyes,
Which we have gazed upon,
Which our hands have handled,
Of the WORD OF LIFE;
For the life was manifested,
And we have seen it,
And bear witness,
And show unto you
That ETERNAL LIFE
Which was with the Father,
And was manifested unto us.

In such marvelous words does the beloved disciple portray the Person of Him who is "the Christ of God." Let this then suffice for an introduction to this volume. They give us some insight into the excellency of knowledge of Jesus Christ our Lord; naming His eternal name; proclaiming His eternal ancestry; showing us the mystery of His ineffable Person; introducing us into the fullness of His love; giving us a glimpse of His glorious light; exhibiting Him as the fountainhead of life; demonstrating to us the absolute certainty of the things made known concerning Him, so that there might not be on any mind the shadow of a doubt concerning either His grace or His glory.

Then, after the wondrous enumeration which He has thus given, the apostle thus announces the meaning and bearing of all this upon our own Christian life — the life which begins in believing the record which God has given of His Son:

"THAT WHICH WE HAVE SEEN AND HEARD DECLARE WE UNTO YOU, THAT YE ALSO MAY HAVE FELLOWSHIP WITH US: AND TRULY OUR FELLOWSHIP IS WITH THE FATHER, AND WITH HIS SON JESUS CHRIST. AND THESE THINGS WRITE WE UNTO YOU, THAT YOUR JOY MAY BE FULL."

For nothing less than the fullness of joy is meant to be the portion of him who believeth that Jesus is the Christ, the Son of God; and nothing short of walking in the light of God ought to be the life of him who has received this Christ, and in receiving Him, has become a son of Him of whom it is written, 'God is light, and in Him no darkness at all.'

THE GRANGE, Nov. 1873

WHAT IS HIS NAME?

Proverbs 30:4 "…and what is His Son's name, if thou canst tell?

Psalms 72:17 "His name shall endure forever: His name shall be continued as long as the sun: and men shall be blessed in Him: All nations shall call Him blessed."

Acts 4:12 "Neither is there salvation in any other: For there is none other name under heaven given among men, whereby we must be saved."

Psalms 145:21 "…Let all flesh bless His Holy name." Psalms 148:13 "…His name alone is excellent." Psalms 105:3 "…Glory Ye in His name." Psalms 103:1 "All that is within me, Bless His Holy name."

And the other songwriter wrote:
"My gracious Master and my God, assist me to proclaim, to spread through all the earth abroad, the honors of Thy name."
Again: "There is a name I love to hear, I love to sing His worth, it sounds like music in my ears, the sweetest name on earth."
Again: "Oh for a thousand tongues to sing my great redeemer's praise..."

There is one name that will last when all others shall have died out; and that name is connected with blessing.

He came into the world on purpose to bless sinners. To bless sinners, He parted with everything:

> *"Though He was rich yet for your sakes He became Poor that you through His poverty might be made rich."*

He was incarnate blessing. He is the ever-blessing One. Our text, (Psalms 72) makes mention of a glorious "Him". And it is through this "Him" that all blessings come!

He is the storehouse of all conceivable good, "and of His fullness have all we received, and Grace for Grace."

No man is ever blessed until he comes to be connected with this "Glorious Him," but in this "Him" I am blessed.

"Blessed is he whose transgressions are forgiven, whose sin is covered. Blessed is the man unto whom the Lord will not impute sin."

Oh, I am blessed in "Him." When a little child of God realizes his union to "Him," he feels so blessed that he does not know of anything that could make him more blessed than he is.

I am always satisfied with Him, I am triumphant in Him, and rejoicing in Him, and in Him I am blessed. Where are you this afternoon, you "blessed" men and women?

Come and enjoy your blessedness; don't be ashamed to be happy, break through the rules of decorum in your church tombs, and express your joy in the sanctuary of the dead.

The old saints were known to have sung so loudly of the joy of their hearts that even their enemies said, "then said they among the heathen, The Lord hath done great things for them: The Lord hath done great things for us; whereof we are glad." (Psalms 126:2-3)

Man shall be blessed in Him: this "Him" is the "Him" of the multitudes. He is the blesser of innumerable myriads of men that He purchased on the cross.

Psalms 72:17 says, 'Men shall be blessed in Him'. This indicates length of time. Men have been blessed in Him for centuries, dispensations, oh how much deeper, how long, and in how many ways we have been blessed in Him! Blessed to the highest degree.

His name removed the curse! No curse abides; only blessings abide! Hallelujah! He lifted from the elect world the weight of the eternal curse! He bore away my sin into the wilderness. But oh, What is His name?

'Men shall be blessed in Him.' Don't ever think that the success of this "Him" depends upon you, that it is in your power to prevent Him from accomplishing almighty purposes of love.

Do not think that by refusing His invitation, you will thwart Him and defeat the purpose of God. No, no, the king's wedding feast shall be furnished with guests. "He" shall make men willing in the day of His power, turning them from darkness to light, and from the power of sin and Satan unto God.

Psalms 72 says, 'His name shall endure forever.'

Webster's dictionary says "name" is a word constituting the distinctive designation of some person or thing. "Name" is the embodiment of a reputation, the spiritual nature of essence." And so it is with the name which is above every name and before which every knee shall bow.

A name uttered more, written more, sung more than any in all the world. There are over 220 names in scripture given of this "Him" of the text, 'whose name shall endure forever.' As we review His name, you will see Him in His glorious person, character, offices and qualities. Through His name, we are helped to know Him more intimately. His very name is vital, powerful, revealing and all important.

I would have you note that this "What's His Name"...This name of His will not go away! This "Him" of Psalms 72:17 has an eternal name! "His name shall endure forever." "His name" is the imperishable name. "His name" shall be perpetuated to everlasting. His worthy name shall be chanted by the Church while the eons of time pile themselves one on top of another. 'His Name' has endured the attack of Heathenism with the classic Greeks and the power of Imperial Rome.

Bibles have been burned by the thousands, men have been burned at the stake. Modernist have called Him a bastard, the liberals have attempted to discredit His name. His own disciples often lived as if "His Name" were but a "passing fancy". But "His Name" shall endure forever! But "His Name" will not fade, "His name" will not fail, "His Name" will not flee.

I tell you as long as there is a sinner on this earth who has been reclaimed by omnipotent grace, "His Name" shall endure...As long as there breathes a "chief of sinners" who has washed himself in the fountain filled with blood, opened for sin and for uncleanness...As long as there exists a Christian who has put his faith in "Him" and found in "Him" his delight, his refuge, his stay, his shield, his song, and his joy, there will be no fear that "His Name" will cease to be heard. As long as there is a sinner who has tasted that "He" is gracious, has manifestations of His love, sights of His face, whispers of His mercy, assurances of His affection, promises of His grace, hopes of His blessing, we will not cease to honor "His name".

Why should the sinner cease to sing His praise, the stones would sing, the hills would be an orchestra, the mountains would skip like rams and the little hills like lambs. And should these be silent, the sun would begin the worthy chant of "His Name"...The moon would play her silver harp...And the night wind sweetly sing "His Name". The stars would dance to His praise. The great ocean tides would crash against the shores shouting, "Thou art the glorious "Him"... great is Thy Majesty and infinite Thy Power. How shall "His Name" ever be forgotten — it is painted on the skies, it is written on the floods. The winds whisper it; the tempests howl it; the seas chant it, the stars shine it, the beast low it; the thunders proclaim it; the earth shouts it... and heaven echoes it.

"His Name" shall endure forever because He is the Author of an immortal book. And in this immortal book He is its subject: He is in it from cover to cover. It declares "Him" the "Him" of prophecy, the "Him" of history, the "Him" of experience, and the "Him" of coming glory. The Old Testament cries, "Behold He comes". The four gospels cry, "Behold He dies". The book of Acts follows with "Behold He lives". The Epistles join the chorus with "Behold He saves". The revelations complete this chorus with "Behold He reigns". He comes, He dies, He lives, He saves, and He reigns. Every part of this immortal book is meant to teach us who He is! He is everywhere to be found in the promises, in the predictions, in the types and emblems of this immortal book.

In "Genesis" He is the seed of the woman. In "Exodus" He is the Passover Lamb. In "Leviticus" He is our High Priest. In "Numbers" He is the pillar of cloud by day and the pillar of fire by night. In "Joshua" He is the Captain of our salvation. In "Judges" He is our

Judge and Lawgiver. In "Ruth" He is our Kingsman-Redeemer. In 1st and 2nd Samuel He is our Trusted Prophet. In "Kings" and "Chronicles" He is our Reigning King. In "Ezra" He is our Faithful Scribe. In "Nehemiah" He is the Rebuilder of the broken walls of our lives. In "Ester" He is our Mordecai. In "Job" He is our Ever-Living Redeemer. In "Psalms" He is the Lord, Our Shepherd. In "Proverbs" and "Ecclesiastes" He is our wisdom. He was "Solomon's" altogether Lovely One. He was "Isaiah's" Child King, Son of a virgin, with shoulders strong enough to bear the government. He was "Jeremiah's" Branch of Righteousness. He was "Ezekiel's" plant of renown, The True Shepherd. He was "Daniel's" stone cut without hands; He was the fourth Man in the fiery furnace. He was to "Joel" the hope of the people. To "Obadiah" the deliverance upon Mt. Zion. To "Micah" the turning again to God. He was the one "Nahum" saw upon the mountains publishing peace. He was the Anointed of whom "Habakkuk" sang as going forth for salvation. He was the true Zerubbabel of "Haggis's" world whose hands laid the foundation of the Church, and His hands shall also finish it.

He Himself is the dawn of the day when holiness shall be upon the bells of the horses, as "Zachariah" foretold. He was the "Sun of Righteousness" of "Malachi's" dream. In "Matthew" He was the Messiah. In "Mark" He was the Wonder-Worker. In "Luke" He was the Son of Man. In "John" He was the Son of God. In "Acts" He was the Holy Spirit working among men. In "Romans" He was the Justifier. In "1st and 2nd Corinthians" He was The Sanctifier. In "Galatians" He was the Redeemer from the curse of the law. In "Ephesians" He was The Christ of unreachable riches. In "Philippians" He is the God who supplieth all our needs. In "Colossians" He was the Fullness of the Godhead bodily. In "1st and 2nd Thessalonians" He was our soon coming King. In "1st and 2nd Timothy" He was the Mediator between God and man. In "Titus" He was the Faithful Pastor. In "Philemon" He was the Friend of the oppressed. In "Hebrews" He was the Blood of the everlasting covenant. In "James" He was the Lord who raised the sick. In "1st and 2nd Peter" He was the Chief Shepherd who soon shall appear. In "1st, 2nd and 3rd John" He was love. In "Jude" He was the Lord coming with ten thousands of saints. In "Revelations" He was our King of Kings and Lord of Lords.

He is the Living Head of an undying family. His family finds in His death their significance, in His life their example, in His cross their redemption, and in His resurrection their hope. In this large family there are many of differing occupations, but to an "artist" He is The Altogether Lovely! To an "Architect" He is The Chief Cornerstone. To an "Astronomer" He is The Sun of Righteousness. To a "Baker" He is The Living Bread. To a "Banker" He is The Hidden Treasure. To a "Biologist" He is Life. To a "Carpenter" He is The Sure Foundation. To a "Doctor" He is a Great Physician. To an "Educator" He is The Great Teacher. To a "Farmer" He is The Sower and The Lord of the harvest. To a "Florist" He is The Lily of the Valley and Rose of Sharon. To a "Geologist" He is the Rock of Ages. To a "Jeweler" He is The Pearl of great price. To a

"Philosopher" He is The Wisdom of God. To a "Christian" He is the Son of The Living God, Savior and Lord.

He is our kindest Friend. He is our unwearied Benefactor. He is our patient Teacher. His wisdom is our guide. His power is our defense. His sympathy is our consolation. His approval is our reward. His salvation is our highest hope. He is the Sun who enlightens us. He is the Physician who heals us. He is the Wall of Fire that defends us. He is the Friend who comforts us. He is the Pearl who enriches us. He is the Ark who supports us. He is the Rock who sustains us. He is the True Deliverer. He is Prophet, Priest, and King. He is the White and Ruddy one. He is The Lion and The Lamb. He is The Servant and the Lord. He is the True Scapegoat, The True Brazen Serpent. He is My Mercy Seat. He is My Joy and My Comfort. His blood is my pardon, His Righteousness is my justification. His Strength is my support; His Promises are my cheer. His Grace keeps me; His Power presents me faultless, His Bond is love and His Burden is light. When I fall, He lifts me up. When I fail, He forgives me. When I am weak, He is strong. When I am lost, He is my way. When I am afraid, He is my courage. When I stumble, He steadies me. When I am hurt, He heals me. When I am broken, He mends me. When I am blind, He leads me. When I am hungry, He feeds me. When I am persecuted, He shields me! When I face loss, He provides for me. When I face death, He carries me home. His ways are right, His word is eternal, His Will is unchanging and His Mind is on me. He is everything for every elect, everywhere, every time and every way. Since He is The Way, there is no other. Since He is The Truth, everything else is a lie. Since He is The Life, everything apart from Him is death. He is Architect of the universe and Manager of all times. He is unmoved, unchanged, undefeated and never undone. He was bruised and brought healing. He was pierced and eased pain. He was Servant and brought freedom. He was dead and brought life. The world cannot understand Him, yet no one can ignore Him. The armies cannot defeat Him. Harod could not kill Him, Nero could not crush Him. The Pharisees could not confuse Him. Hitler could not silence Him. Phil Donahue cannot explain Him! The new age cannot replace Him. And the "salvation by works people" cannot control Him. He is Keeper of the creation and The Creator of all He keeps.

He had no servants, yet they called Him master. He had no degree, yet they called Him teacher. He had no medicines, yet they called him healer. He had no army, yet kings feared Him. He won no military battles, yet he conquered the world. He committed no crime, yet they crucified Him. He was buried in a tomb, yet He lives today.

But what is His name? His Name is Jehovah, God, The Son of God, His Name is Wonderful, Counselor, Mighty God, Prince of Peace, Rose of Sharon, Lily of the Valley, Bright and Morning Star. He is Bread of heaven, Water of Life, The Door, The Truth, The Way, and The Life. He is Alpha and Omega, Beginning and Ending, First and Last. He is The Resurrection, the Key Holder. Reverend and Holy is His Name. He is the Image of The Invisible God, The First Begotten of every creature. He is Head of The Church, The First Born from the dead. He is The Pearl from Paradise. He is The Gem from The Holy Land. He is Time's Choicest Theme. He is Life's Strongest Cord. His Blessed Name is like honey to the taste, like harmony to the ear, help to the soul and hope to the heart.

He precedes all others in priority; He exceeds all others in His Superiority, and He succeeds all others in His finality. He is Master of the mighty. He is Captain of the conquerors. He is Head of the heroes. He is Leader of the legislators. He is the overseer of the overcomers. He is The Governor of the governors. He is the Prince of the princes. He is The Owner, for He is Lord!

Even though He did not put His signature in the sunset...He is still The Owner! Though He did not put His mark on the meadow, He is still The Owner. Though He did not carve His initials in the side of the mountains, He is still The Owner. Even though He did not put a brand on the cattle of a thousand hills, He is still The Owner. He did not take out a copyright on the songs the birds sing, He is still The Owner.

He overrules all mortal things; He directs the movement of the stars; He rules the armies of heaven. His kingdom rules over all and of His Dominion there shall be no end. Here is His claim, "All power is given unto Me".

He came down the stairway of heaven, was born in Bethlehem, grew up in Nazareth, was baptized in Jordan, was tempted in the wilderness, performed miracles by the roadside, healed multitudes without medicine, and made no charges for His services.

He conquered everything that came up against Him, went up to Calvary and died there. Then he went down into the grave and there cleaned out the grave and made it a pleasant place to wait for the Resurrection. Then on the third day He got up with the power of His Omnipotence.

Men have been trying to wrestle His power from Him all these years. But you cannot destroy Him. What are you going to use for power? All power belongs to Him. If you try to destroy Him by fire, He will refuse to burn; if you try to destroy Him by water, He will walk on the water. If you try to destroy Him by a strong wind, the tempest will lick His hand and lay down at His feet. If you try to destroy Him with a law, you will find no fault in Him. If you put Him in a grave, He will rise. If you try to destroy Him by rejection, it will not be long until you will hear a still small voice saying, "This is the way walk ye in it."

Do you know His name? In Him you have a standing that can never be disputed. A justification that can never be reversed; an inheritance that can never be alienated; a wealth that can never be depleted; a resource that can never be diminished; a bank that can never be closed; a peace that can never be destroyed; a joy that can never be surpassed. A grace that can never be arrested. A strength that can never be weakened. An intercessor who can never be disqualified. A victor who can never be vanished. A resurrection that can never be prevented. A destiny that can never be changed. A hope that can never be disappointed. A glory that can never be dimmed. A relationship that can never be revoked. A righteousness that can never be tarnished. An acceptance that can never be questioned. A title that can never be clouded. A position that can never be invalidated. A life that can never be forfeited.

Let me try to tell you who He is one more time. He is Peace in the valley, He is Peace in the fiery furnace, He is Peace in the lions' den, He is Peace crossing the Red Sea, He is Peace in the time of trouble, He is peace in the day of judgment.

His name is Purifier, Potter, Prince, and Propitiation. His name is Physician and Potentate. His name is Root, Refuge, Rock, Redeemer, Redemption, Righteousness, and Ransom. He is rivers of living water in a dry place. He is a Savior, a Shepherd, Son of David, Son of God, Star of Jacob, Shiloh, Sun of Righteousness, and Sanctification.

He is a Teacher, a Tower, and a Testator. He is the Tree of Life and the Truth. He is Minister, Messenger, Message, Mediator, Messiah, and my Mighty God. He is a Light in a dark place; He is the Light of the world; He is Lord of all; He is Love divine; He is longevity, He is a Lawgiver, and He is my Lord. He is a Daystar, a Day Spring, a Daysman, He is the desire of all nations, and He is my desire. He is an advocate; He is ancient of days and He is my amen. He is the Chief Cornerstone; He is the Captain of my salvation, He is a counselor; and He is my consolation. He is a Forerunner, a finisher, a First, a Fortress, a Fountain, a Friend of sinners, a friend that sticketh closer than a brother. He is the Galilean; He is Goodness; He is Gentleness; and He is God.

Let me hear you say His name — Jesus, Jesus, Jesus. Let all heaven and earth proclaim — Kings and kingdoms will all pass away, but there is something about that name.

Oh, but if you do not know His name, you have no priest to atone or intercede. You have no fountain to wash away your guilt. No passover blood which you can sprinkle on your lintel. No shepherd to tend you, no king to help you, no providence to work your good. No advocate to plead your case and cause in heaven. No representative to stand up yonder and represent you.

Without knowing Him, His name, you are a body without a head, a miserable orphan with no father, a widow soul without a husband, you are without a savior. Without a friend in heaven, without a virtue of His great sacrifice, without merit of His atoning blood. Without Christ, your transgressions are not buried...without Christ there shall be none to wipe away the tears from your eyes. Without Christ your religious acts are vanity, without Christ your church goings are a form of slavery. Your prayers are empty wind. Your good deeds are nothing but camouflage to hide your base iniquities. Your profession is a whited sepulchre. Your religion is dead, corrupt, a stench, a nuisance, before God. There is nothing for God to see that can possibly please Him. You moral people are as lost as the immoral. You will be damned with the prostitute.

Philippians 2:10 That at the name of Jesus every knee should bow, of things in heaven, and things in earth, and things under the earth.

Earth's long rebellion shall soon come to a perpetual end. Each spoiler shall be spoiled, each conqueror conquered, each prison opened, each boaster silenced, each blasphemer confounded, each antichrist smitten, each rival throne overturned and at the name of Jesus every knee shall bow, of things in heaven, and things in earth, and things under the earth and the Great "Christ" shall take to Himself His Great Power and Reign".

"All Hail the power of Jesus name! Let angels prostrate fall, bring forth the royal diadem, and crown Him Lord of All!"

CONTENTS

CHAPTER 1

THE DIVINE PURPOSE

'THERE came a voice from heaven, saying, This is my beloved son, in whom I am well pleased' (Matthew 3:17; Mark 1:11; Luke 3:22).

Let us read these words as the utterance of the divine mind concerning Him who is called 'the Christ of God' (Luke 9:20), or 'the Lord's Christ (Luke 2:26), or 'Christ the Lord' (Luke 2:11). Let us hear from them also the *divine* estimate of Him whom man refused to love, who was 'despised and rejected by men,' who 'came unto His own, and His own received Him not'.

That peculiar name, 'the Christ of God', embodies in it not so much 'the *thoughts* of God as THE THOUGHT of God, the summing up of all His thoughts, the one great idea, the root and center of all others, containing in it that which it will require eternity to evolve; for He to whom that thought pertains is the Alpha and the Omega, the beginning and the ending, the first and the last. (Rev.1,8,11,17)

The great thought, thus embodied in the person of Christ, concerns us. It does not name us, or our earth, and yet it has respect to both; and in the history of this Christ, our everlasting history is contained. The right knowledge of Him, then, must be of infinite importance to us. To know Him rightly must be our very life; to know Him wrongly, or not to know Him at all, must be very death.

This great thought of God contains in it all that is worthy of the name of TRUTH; and especially does it contain the highest form of truth, or that which we call WISDOM, for wisdom is but the purest and highest form of truth; and the knowledge of the highest form of truth must bring with it the highest form of light, and peace, and liberty.

'We know the truth, and the truth makes us free' (John 8:32): for all error is bondage, it may be of the mind or the conscience or the heart; all error is darkness and disquietude. It is truth that illuminates and gladdens. The Christ, as the Truth, liberates us, as the Truth He gives peace, as the Truth He enlightens. For Him there can be no substitute to man. The fullness deposited in Him is to be found nowhere else. He only is 'the WISDOM of God,' and it is that Wisdom with which man has to do. He needs it, and it was appointed for Him. When Jesus said, 'Learn of me,' He spoke as the Wisdom of God, offering to reveal to us that wisdom in which rest is contained for the weary. For true wisdom is true rest, and divine wisdom is divine rest.

But this wisdom expresses itself in a *purpose*. That purpose is the result of thought, and the embodiment of the highest wisdom. God's purpose in regard to man and man's world is wrapped up in 'the Christ of God.' This is called 'the mystery of His will, according to HIS GOOD PLEASURE WHICH HE HATH PURPOSED in Himself, that in the dispensation of the fullness of the times He might gather in one all things in Christ, both which are in heaven and which are on earth, even in Him, in whom we also have obtained an inheritance, being PREDESTINATED ACCORDING TO THE PURPOSE of Him who worketh all things after THE COUNCIL OF HIS OWN WILL, that we should be to the praise of His Glory' (Eph. 1:8-12).

God's purpose, then, takes definite form in Christ, and all the various parts of that infinite purpose are connected with Him. The purpose is, like the Purposer, eternal; but the form of it belongs to time. The first announcement of the purpose was in Paradise to our first parents. The first visible unfolding of it was at Bethlehem, and seemed nothing but a small fragment of human history — the birth of a poor Jewish child in a southern village of Palestine, under the open sky. They who saw this did not complain about it, nor read in it anything great or glorious. They could not have fathomed it, even had they tried to do so; but they did not try, because it seemed too insignificant to touch upon anything but the interests of an obscure Galilean family. Angels might see something of its hidden magnificence; man did not. It was a seed, the growth and fruit of which were to spread over the universe and reach on into the ages to come; but the seed was unrecognized by human eyes and no one saw in it the greatest of all the great things had come to pass from the beginning of time. In its underdeveloped glory it lay as a common piece of Jewish village-story, none understanding the difference between that birth and any other birth that had taken place; none reading in it the first visible revelation of Jehovah's eternal purpose, nor imagining the wonders of grace, and power, and wisdom which were wrapped up in it, and to emerge from it in the fullness of time. Who among the ten thousands of Israel connected with that child the destinies of the universe? And how many, even of believing Israelites, gathered around that stony cradle, to sing the ancient song they knew so well: 'Unto us a child is born, unto us a Son is given; and the government shall be upon His shoulder: and His name shall be called, Wonderful, Counselor, the Mighty God, the everlasting Father, Prince of Peace'? (Isa. 9:6.) His mother might 'keep all these things, and ponder them in her heart' (Luke 2:19); but how little did even she comprehend the breadth and length, the heighth and depth, of the infinite plan thus visibly announced! Yet in that cradle was deposited *the eternal purpose,* and that mother's arms encompassed that *purpose* as they clasped the babe on whose history all history was to turn. It was the sin of man that drew out this great purpose into shape; for always has God made use of human failure for revealing more of Himself and His truth. There has been a previous failure of creaturehood; but the purpose was not connected with that, nor did that failure draw out any manifestation of God, or any announcement of His purpose. For the fullness of the times did that purpose wait, hidden in the councils of the Godhead, yet ready to come forth when the exigencies of the second race of creaturehood furnished the long waited for opportunity. Now that the instability of creaturehood had been twice over demonstrated, the needed deliverance comes; and the purpose of the deliverance is embodied in the Child of Bethlehem, the Word made flesh. God becometh man, that man may not only be replaced in his former state, but lifted up to a higher level — 'made partaker of the divine nature.' Creaturehood has been twice broken to pieces; now God steps into accomplish these two things: (1) to lay a foundation for it that it shall never fall again; (2) to impart to it an excellency such as it could not have otherwise possessed. Both these ends are accomplished by linking together the divine and the human in a way such as could not before have been conceived possible — by the Son of God becoming bone of *our* bone, and flesh of *our* flesh, that thus *we* might be members of *His* body, of His flesh and His bones.

That 'we are His offspring' (Acts 16:28) was always true; but now it is doubly so — true in a higher sense and form; and thus also is the great truth of creaturehood's subsistence in God not only more fully manifested, but made a yet truer and more glorious thing; and through the Christ of God, we find a newer and more blessed reality in the fact that 'in Him we live, and move, and have our being.' There is nothing here of the mystical dream of 'absorption in Godhead;' but there is something more real, as well as more high and blessed. 'I in them, and Thou in me, that they may be made perfect in one, and that the world may know that Thou hast sent me, and hast loved them, as Thou hast loved me' (John 17:23).

Thus, in delivering and elevating us, He reveals Himself and brings forth all the glories of His character, as well as all the resources of His being. He descends that we may ascend. In *descending,* He manifests Himself, for God cannot *ascend*; and it is only in *descending* that He can reveal all His riches of grace and power. It is for a man to ascend, and in ascending receive a glory which does not belong to him. In it, for God to descend, and in descending to unveil the glory which but for this descent would have been hidden not only from man, but from the universe. 'Glory to God' had been sung before, when the morning stars sang together, and the sons of God shouted for joy; but not until now could 'glory to God IN THE HIGHEST' be sung by either men or angels.

Thus the purpose of God was to reveal Himself in 'the Christ' and in so revealing Himself, to lift up fallen man into blessedness and glory. It was also to bring forth from the ruins of humanity a higher and greater order of creaturehood, which by its connection with incarnate Godhead might be secured against the possibility of fall. 'For as we have borne the image of the EARTHLY, we shall also bear the imagine of the HEAVENLY' (1 Cor. 15:49). And these are words of profound import which declare this process of elevation: 'The first Adam was made a living soul; the last Adam was made a quickening spirit. Howbeit that was not first which is spiritual, but that which is natural; and afterward that which is spiritual. The first man is of the earth, earthly; the second man is the Lord from heaven. As is the earthly, such are they that are earthly; and as is the heavenly, such are they also that are heavenly' (1 Cor. 15:45-48).

Such are the objects of the divine purpose as taking visible shape in 'the Christ of God' — 'God manifest in the flesh.' All truth is here; all wisdom is here; all perfection is here; and in connection with these, 'the exceeding riches of the grace of God.' This is 'the eternal purpose which He purposed in Christ Jesus our Lord' (Eph. 3:11); the purpose to which the apostle so often refers — (1) in connection with 'this present evil age' (Gal.1:4); (2) in connection with 'the age to come' (Heb. 6:5); (3) in connection with 'the ages to come' (Eph. 2:7). Here is the fountainhead of all things in heaven and in earth — the moving, impelling, regulating, controlling, spring of all that has been witnessed here in ages past, or that shall be witnessed hereafter, when the full spreading out of the unsearchable riches of the Christ shall take place, in ways and in regions to us unknown, and by us unconceived and inconceivable: for the far-ranging and universe-filling glory yet to come forth from that wondrous center is not only something which eye hath not seen, nor ear heard, but which hath not entered into the heart of man.

To bring a fair world out of nothing was God's creation-purpose, and the first chapters of Genesis reveal its accomplishment. But to bring a fairer and more stable world out of creation's ruin, a nobler and more perfect race out of the corruption of that which had fallen, was God's redemption-purpose; and of the means to the accomplishment of this, as well as of the accomplishment itself, the whole Bible is the record. The burden of that record is the history of the Christ of God. For 'Christ is all, and in all' (Col 3:11) — THE ALL, AND THE IN ALL — containing everything, filling everything; at once the vessel of fullness and the fullness of the vessel; as the Christ, distinct from, yet one with, Godhead; distinct from, yet one with Creaturehood; God over all, blessed forever, in whom dwelleth all the fullness of the Godhead bodily; God manifest in the flesh, yet also the man Christ Jesus, who took upon Him not the nature of angels, but the seed of Abraham; becoming poor that we might be made rich; emptying Himself that He might fill us; and ascending up to heaven 'that He might fill all things. For all the fullness of the universe is His, and the glory of all things, celestial and terrestrial, is the outflowing of the glory of the Christ of God.

Therefore is He called the 'image of the invisible God' (Col. 1-15), so that he that hath seen Him hath seen the Father; and yet 'the firstborn of every creature' (Col. 1:15): 'For by Him were all things created, that are in heaven, and that in earth visible and invisible whether they be thrones, or dominions, or principalities, or powers: all things were created by Him, and for Him; and He is before all things, and by Him all things consist; and He is the head of the body, the Church: the beginning, the firstborn from the dead; that in all things He might have the preeminence. For it pleased the Father that in Him should all fullness dwell' (Col. 1:16-19).

Thus 'the incarnation' is no afterthought; no change of mind; no revocation of one purpose in order to introduce another, because of something that had unexpectedly given way; but the carrying out of the great original purpose, dating from eternity, whose fulfillment or fulfillments, with all the conflicting events (contingencies, as men call them) evoking these fulfillments, were present to the eternal mind from the beginning, in connection with that plan, which assumed and provided for what man calls the unforeseen and fortuitous; nay, whose most important unfoldings are drawn out by that which seems to us especially fortuitous and incapable of being foreseen.

That creaturehood should, by reason of inherent weakness, be incapable of standing alone, does not seem to us at all a likelihood, far less a certainty; and God has, by two successive falls (of angels and men), proved to us, as out of the mouth of two witnesses, the innate helplessness of the creature apart from the Creator. But the divine plan did not require to wait the issue of this double 'experiment,' not to be guided and moulded by the issue of this double demonstration. It took its shape not from what might or might not become fact, according to human calculation, but from what was known from the beginning to Him who seeth the end from the beginning; with whom there is nothing uncertain or contingent; to Him 'of whom, and through whom, and to whom are all things,' whose judgments are unsearchable, and whose ways past finding out (Rom. 11:33).

'There is none good but one' and there is none unchangeable or infallible but one; and the God who created all things by Jesus Christ 'is the God *only* wise.' This wisdom, and immutability, and goodness belong not to the creature, but to the Creator. To become partakers of these, the creature must be linked to the Creator by a bond far beyond that of creaturehood; a bond which could only be framed by means of 'incarnation' — God coming down to us and taking on flesh, that we might be lifted up to Him and made 'partakers of the divine nature.' Thus, and thus only, is creaturehood preserved from any third or future fall, and established forever, in spite of its inherent helplessness because of a divine foundation.

All this comprehended in that purpose whereby the Christ of God is constituted alike the foundation and the head of the universe — 'the beginning and the ending, the first and the last.'

Yet in all this there is no contradiction to the divine declarations concerning 'the grace of God.' The great purpose does not interfere with the fact that 'God so loved the world, that He gave His only begotten Son, that whosoever believeth in Him should not perish, but have everlasting life' (John 3:16). Some seem to think that they cannot reconcile an eternal purpose regarding 'the Christ' with a love to man, the sinner — a love which did not come into being until man fell, nay, the existence of which was contingent upon his sinning. But to reconcile such a purpose and such a love is no more difficult than to reconcile the entrance of sin with the power of a holy Being who was altogether able to prevent that entrance had

He willed to do so. And, indeed, almost all the theological or metaphysical questions and perplexities with which men have engaged for ages run themselves up into the one question — why did a holy and almighty God allow sin to enter the world? The true answer to that one question is the answer to a thousand others. The fact of *sin's existence* is the real difficulty and stumbling block. Admit its existence, and we must admit that its admission was no accident, far less a necessity; and, if neither an accident nor a necessity, it must have been the result of a purpose, founded upon a far wider basis than we can comprehend — a basis which takes in the bearing of (1) sin repressed or prevented, (2) sin admitted, (3) sin overruled, not upon the one sinner only, or upon the one world where the sin was committed, but upon the universe. The divine purpose regarding the admission of sin for a reason and its subsequent removal by a process of mingled love and righteousness, assumes that the absolute repression or prevention of sin was *not the best thing for the universe,* for the glory of the Creator; but that its entrance and ultimate removal were issues infinitely more beneficial to the universe and glorying to God. The number of smaller but yet glorious ends comprised in and subserved by this entrance and removal is altogether beyond calculation and conception; and the manifestation of God thus accomplished far outweighs the evils arising from the introduction of sin. But whether we are prepared or not to rest here, and be satisfied with such a solution, we must silence our questionings by divine declarations such as these: In this was manifested the love of

God toward us, because that God sent His only begotten Son into the world that we might live through Him. Herein is love, not that we loved God, but that God loved us, and sent His Son to be the propitiation for our sins' (1 John 4:7,10). 'God, who is rich in mercy, for His great love wherewith He loved us, even when we were dead in sins, hath quickened us together with Christ' (Eph. 2:4). Insofar as man is concerned, that purpose reveals itself in love; and the proclamation which it has made both to earth and heaven is, 'GOD IS LOVE.' Here let us rest amid our manifold perplexities. There is no doubt now as to this. The coming of the Christ of God has settled all questions as to this; and we may sit down in peace beneath the shadow of the cross, seeing in that cross the great demonstration of the righteous love of God.

That love is not indeed the vague feeling of kindness or good nature, or indifference to sin, which many ascribe to God. It is something more true, more real, more worthy of God, and more suited to the case of man. It is love whose very nature is abhorrence of sin; love which can only come forth to the sinner in some way consistent with that abhorrence; nay, which carries out its purpose of love in order to show this changeable hatred. This hatred of sin is not mere general dislike of what is evil; but it is that judicial opposition to it, which can only be met or satisfied by the payment of the penalty due by the transgressor. Law demands the penalty, but it is satisfied if it is paid by a substitute; for thus all the ends of holy government are completely fulfilled. The law is magnified and made honorable; yet the sinner is delivered, and God can, without encroachment upon righteousness, bestow His forgiving love upon those who had merited only displeasure and condemnation.

This love of God shines in the face of One who is not simply Savior, but *Substitute;* of One who, by His suffering the Just for the unjust, has not merely demonstrated the reality of the love, but made it to issue forth, like the pure river of the water of life, from the throne of God, the seat of judgment and holiness.

Such is the divine purpose — the purpose of the God only wise — yet the purpose of Him who is the 'Lord God, merciful and gracious, forgiving iniquity, transgression, and sin.'

In this purpose we discover that which is to be the foundation stone, not only for man and man's world, but for the universe: for God, in His scheme for redeeming His Church, has taken in the whole range of being, far and near, and made provision for all His vast creation, so that that which is done for man bears more or less directly on everything which God has 'created and made.'

In what way this is to affect heaven and holy beings or regions beyond earth, we know not. This we know that it is written: 'Having made peace through the blood of HIS CROSS, BY HIM TO RECONCILE ALL THINGS UNTO HIMSELF; BY HIM, I SAY, WHETHER THEY BE THINGS IN EARTH OR THINGS IN HEAVEN' (Col. 1:20). Nay, still further, we know that it is written concerning this 'mystery of His will:' 'According to His good pleasure which He hath purposed in Himself,' — 'that, in the dispensation of the fullness of times, He might GATHER TOGETHER IN ONE ALL THINGS IN CHRIST, BOTH WHICH ARE IN HEAVEN AND WHICH ARE ON EARTH, EVEN IN HIM' (Eph. 1:10).

CHAPTER 2

THE FULLNESS OF THE CHRIST

There are three special names or designations of Him who in the eternal purpose is presented to us as the Christ. The *first* of these is THE WISDOM; and the divine description of this we have in the eighth chapter of Proverbs. The *second* is THE WORD; and it is of this that the Evangelist John speaks in his first chapter. The third is THE SON; and of him the Apostle Paul writes in the first chapter of the Epistle to the Hebrews.

Each of these three takes us back into the past eternity. The Wisdom is eternal; the Word is eternal; the Son is eternal.

As the eternal *Wisdom*, He possessed all that we call knowledge or truth, in every form and every kind. In Him were 'hid all the treasures or wisdom and knowledge' (Col 2:3). He was the Wisdom of God; and because He was so, 'He made unto us wisdom' (1 Cor. 1:30), so that we are 'wise in Christ' (1 Cor. 4:10). As the Wisdom, He is the Truth; not simply the depositary or dispenser of the truth, but Himself the Truth as He said, 'I am the way, and THE TRUTH, and the life' (John 14:6).

As the eternal *Word,* He is the revealer of the mind of Godhead; for as it is by words that we come into contact with the invisible mind, and know the thoughts and feelings within, so it is by Him, as the Word, that we are made acquainted with the mind of God. It is through Him that God speaks to us, and it is in Him that God shows us what He is. 'He that hath seen me hath seen the Father'; without Him, the character of God would have been to us a blank, or utter darkness. In the beginning was the Word, and the Word was with God, and the Word was God; the same was in the beginning with God.' As the *Wisdom*, and the *Word*, He is the *Light* of the world (John 8:12); 'for in Him was life, AND THE LIFE was the *light* of men' (John 1:4). As the Revealer of Godhead, the utterer of the divine mind, He is both the light and the life of men: that life and light which speak to us of the holy love of God, and invite us to become partakers of that love.

As the eternal Son, He is 'the brightness of Jehovah's glory, and the express image of His person' (Heb. 1:2); distinct from the Father, yet one with the Father; holding filial fellowship with the Father, and inviting us to enter into that same fellowship and relationship as sons; as the Son, giving to us 'the spirit of adoption, whereby we cry, Abba, Father' (Rom. 8:15); and making us not only children, but heirs of the inheritance, 'heirs of God, and joint-heirs with Christ' (Rom. 8:17).

The unfolding of the divine purpose was through this eternal Wisdom, this eternal Word, and this eternal Son. Thus hath 'God, who commanded the light to shine out of darkness, shined in our hearts, to give the light of the knowledge of the glory of God in the face of Jesus Christ' (2 Cor. 4:6). Thus, too, the 'mystery' is unfolded, into the 'fellowship' of which we enter (Eph 3:9), which from the beginning was hid in God, who created all things by Jesus Christ: to the intent that now, unto the principalities and powers in heavenly places, might be known by the Church the manifold wisdom of God, according to the ETERNAL PURPOSE WHICH HE PURPOSED IN CHRIST JESUS OUR LORD' (Eph. 3:10-11).

In the above passages there are two great truths that fall specifically to be noticed. The first is the divine glory as seen in the face of Christ, and the second is the divine wisdom in connection with the Church. These two are closely linked together. They are the counterparts of each other.

1. *The Glory of God in the face of Jesus Christ.* – Everything connected with the light and the glory is from above; not of man, but of God. For earth has no resources of its own to fall back upon, in its day of darkness and evil. Man can create shadows, but he can dispel none, he can quench light, but cannot create it. The creation of light belongs to God alone.

   And man did quench the light and reduce himself, as well as his world to chaos. As man's earth was, so was man himself, 'without form, and void, and darkness was upon the face of the deep' (Gen.1:3). He is the wreck of a goodly and glorious world: for God did not create him a child of darkness, but of light; the essence of that light being love, and knowledge, and holiness. The curse lighted down upon earth, swept across it, brooded over it, dwelt in it, and still continues to dwell; and in that curse there is confusion, and blackness, and sorrow. For the curse is no mere tempest, fierce but passing. It is a spreading and deepening deluge. Man has let it loose upon himself; but in vain he tries to bid it subside, or turn it into a 'pure river of the water of life, clear as crystal.'

Yet light exists somewhere, and darkness surely is not everlasting. Heaven is not dark, though earth is; and angels are still bright, through devils have lost their purity. There is hope, because there is light — light somewhere.

The source is God Himself; for 'the light dwelleth with Him' (Dan. 2:22). He is light, as truly as He is love; and 'in Him is no darkness at all' (1 John 1:5). He is clothed with light as with a garment, even though He dwelleth, as is said, 'in the thick darkness' (1 Kings 8:12). This God is the fountainhead of light. It was He who commanded the light to shine out of darkness, saying, 'Let there be light, and there was light.' Not merely does He shine *into* us, but He shines *in* us, in our hearts; He kindles a lamp, a sun, within us; nay, He comes into us, and is Himself the Sun. As His gift for quenching of our thirst is not merely a full supply of water from without, but a well of water within, 'springing up into everlasting life' (John 4:14); so that 'put of us there flow rivers of living water' (John 7:37); so His gift for the removal of our darkness is *a sun within us*, filling us with light, and disturbing its radiance around, making us to become 'lights in a world.' He lighted up the *old* creation; He lights up the *new*. In enlightening, He creates us anew; and in creating us anew, He enlightens us. He who lighted up stars and suns lights up souls; and as He loveth to do the one, so no less does He love to do the other. Thus every star in the firmament preaches to us, not merely 'the being of a God,' but His liberality and love; His willingness to give us light; as if He said to us, 'As I live, saith the Lord, I have no pleasure that you should remain in darkness, but rather that ye should become light in the Lord.' And as it needed but a word to light up the universe, so it needs but a word, O man, to light up your whole being!

This light has its center or source in 'the glory of God.' The 'glory' of the outshining perfection of splendor of Godhead, spiritual or material. Of this the Shekinah which dwelleth in the Holy of Holies was expression or symbol; and it is this glory of God that is seen *in the face of Jesus Christ*. That face is radiant with the love of God. 'The Word was made flesh, and dwelt among us; and we beheld His

Glory, the glory as of the only begotten of the Father, full of grace and truth' (John 1:14).

The Christ of God is thus identified with the glory. It is the glory of Godhead; and in it we see God coming down to us in love bringing His love to our very side; embodying that love in our flesh; pouring it into a vessel that we can always have access to — always near and always full. In the face of Jesus Christ, thus radiant with the divine glory, we learn the meaning of the words, 'He that hath seen me hath seen the Father. Believest thou not that I am in the Father, and the Father in me?' (John 14:9-10). In it we find God Himself approaching us as the God of peace and the God of grace, reconciling the world to Himself, not inputting unto men their trespasses; putting an end to all distance, and distrust, and variance; drawing into fellowship; welcoming back His prodigals to home, and heart, and table; giving them the best robe, and providing for them the feast of fat things; nay, bringing them into peculiar nearness through His incarnate Son, and imparting to them a new, more divine, more glorious light than that which they had lost.

'Look unto me' is the message! Look unto me, and behold the glory — the glory of love, the glory of peace, the glory of acceptance in Him in whom we are complete! The 'God of glory' is the 'God of peace' and 'the God of all grace.' The 'glory' and the 'light' are connected with 'the Word made flesh,' and they are seen in His 'face.' That face is the face of Him who, though He was rich, for our sakes became poor, that we by His poverty might be made rich. There is no frown upon that brow. There is no anger in that eye. There is no scorn upon that lip. There are no words of coldness or of repulsion proceeding from that tongue. The whole of that face is lighted up with love, the perfect love which casteth out fear, the love which passeth knowledge, the love which bids the sinner welcome, which invites the touch of the sinner's hand, and the trust of the sinner's heart; for there is no fear, nothing to cause fear, in this love — nothing that is not fitted to remove all fear and awaken all confidence. The brightness of His countenance does not alarm, for all that brightness is upon the side of the sinner. It is no scorching brilliance, but the placid dayspring from on high, the healing light from the Sun of righteousness, of which every ray speaks peace, and in which there is life, and not death, to the sons of men. The 'King of glory' is He who 'receiveth sinners, and eateth with them.'

That which we preach is 'the glorious gospel,' or rather, 'the gospel of the GLORY' (1 Tim. 1:11), the glad tidings concerning the GLORY; for all that GLORY in every part contains the message of forgiveness, and the invitation to life eternal. To gaze upon that GLORY, so full of grace and truth, is to receive into the soul the sunshine which illuminates and warms, which comforts and heals. There is no terror in it. It does not turn our comeliness into corruption (Dan. 10:8), nor make us fall at His feet as dead (Rev. 1:17), nor make us 'hide ourselves in the dust' or in the rocks for 'the glory of His majesty' (Isa. 2:10); it is 'the health of our countenance' (Ps. 42:11), and it is the peace of our souls. It was 'the God of GLORY' that appeared to Abraham when a dark idolater in Chaldea (Acts 7:2); and as that GLORY was to him the mighty attractive, drawing him out of his idolatry and unbelief, so it is still the gracious magnet which draws the sinner from his sin, and wins his heart to God. For though it is holy, it is irresistibly attractive, as was the Son of God in the days of His flesh; though it is righteous, and cannot ally itself with sin, yet in it there is something so suitable and so loving that everyone who truly sees it, sees in it the enemy of terror and doubt. 'On earth peace, and goodwill toward men,' is the substance of the revelation contained in it. 'Help us O Lord, for the GLORY of Thy *name*' (Ps. 79:9) is the cry of everyone who sees and knows it. The GLORY of Jehovah's *name* is the most powerful argument which the sinner can use in drawing near to God; and every other argument is included in it.

2. *The divine wisdom connected with the Church.* – The words of the apostle are very remarkable concerning this. There was a 'mystery,' or secret (for this is the meaning of the word), an

eternal mystery, 'from the beginning hid in God,' not revealed at first, when He 'created all things by Jesus Christ,' and yet wrapped up in that creation-purpose and creation-act, as he says 'hid in God, who created all things by Jesus Christ.' This 'mystery' was not the creation of these heavens and earth, and still more with THE CHURCH. 'The Church' is the great embodiment and exhibition of the divine wisdom. First 'the Christ' was such; then, in connection with Him, the Church. In the person of Christ was the sum of all wisdom; and in the Church, as redeemed by Him, is in another from the sum of wisdom — that wisdom by which angels are to be taught, and from which they have learned, and are yet to learn, more of God than they have learned or can learn from aught else, either on earth or in heaven. It is not 'the Church' without 'the Christ,' nor is it 'the Christ' without 'the Church,' that is to form the wondrous lesson for 'principalities and powers in heavenly places,' but both together: the Christ as the Godman redeeming his Church; the Church as His body, His bride, His chosen and loved from all eternity, redeemed by Him and lifted up by Him out of the lowest condition of evil into the highest seat of heaven, beside Himself, as the royal priesthood, no being receiving from the fullness of His love, but sharing with Him His honor and glory, His crown and throne.

In it the 'manifold wisdom of God' that is to be learned from the Church by the principalities and powers in heavenly places; as if, apart from the Church and its history, the wisdom of God could not have been known even by the angels. Their own history must have taught them much; for the history of a single creature, even for one day, is the revelation of divine wisdom; but all their own wondrous story, both in the case of those who fell and those who stood, could not teach them what the story of the Church has already taught, and shall continue to teach forever.

It might have been said that they learned from the Church the *love* of God, the *power* of God, the *truth* of God, the *righteousness* of God, the *holiness* of God; and some perhaps ask, Why is it *wisdom* alone that is said to be learned in this way and from this source? For this clear reason, that all these other things are comprehended in this wisdom; and the wisdom is so marvelously and so manifoldly manifested in a purpose of plan, whose vast object is to reveal THE WHOLE OF GOD in a way which had not hitherto been done, and which could not have been accomplished save by a fall and a restoration, such as we see in the Church, and in each individual member of that redeemed company, for whom, as for His bride, the Son of God gave Himself.

Angels (and we also) would have known but half the love of God, half the power of God, half the truth and righteousness and holiness of God, without the Church. I speak of *half*, but I might have said, not the half, but the thousandth part of these. For all these have come out in such new light and glory, by means of God's dealings with the fallen, that what was known of them before seems as nothing when compared with what had thus been revealed. The whole fullness of the divine character could have been unfolded, except in connection with the redemption of the fallen. That He loves the holy and the lovable had always been known to angels, but that He can love the unholy and the unlovable could not have been known to them; nay, from His treatment of their lost fellows, when He consigned them to chains irretrievably, it must have been supposed by them that He could not love the unworthy or the sinful, and that there was no possibility of such a thing as grace or mercy to the lost. The divine character was thus left unmanifested, not merely insofar as love was concerned, but also in regard to power, and righteousness, and holiness. That He could love the lost was unknown; that He could love to such an extent, and with such a love as He had done, was still more unknown. Thus His infinitely loving and lovable character was hidden. But the extent of His power and the nature of His righteousness were equally undiscovered. His power in creation was known, but His omnipotence in redemption was only seen in the Church. His righteousness in caring for the righteous and condemning the transgressor was known; but His righteousness in His gracious dealings with the unrighteous, and in delivering the transgressor from his eternal doom, was something which could not have been even imagined before. What a veil was withdrawn from the character of God by the first promise of grace! And what a marvelous illumination of that character was given in the incarnation and crucifixion of the only begotten Son of God! All was love, peace, righteousness, truth, holiness; yet all was WISDOM — profound and unsearchable wisdom, wisdom such as furnished angels with an eternal lesson and an endless song; wisdom such as shall, in the full expanding of its plan, fill heaven and earth, nay, all the universe, with new and glorious light. 'O the depth of the riches, both of the wisdom and knowledge of God! How unsearchable are His judgments, and His ways past finding out! For of Him, and through Him, and to Him are all things; to whom be glory forever.' Let the Church say Amen! Let angels say Amen! Let heaven and earth say Amen! Let all the universe say Amen!

CHAPTER 3

ISRAEL'S MESSIAH THE CHRIST OF THE NEW TESTAMENT

'MESSIAH' — the 'Christ,' the 'Anointed One' — was a well known name in Israel. To many it was no doubt but a sound or name, but to 'them that believed' it was precious; embodying as it did to them, and to their nation, all hope and joy; announcing to them the love which passeth knowledge; and predicting a glory coming, such an eye had not seen nor ear heard.

MESSIAH was Israel's hope; and His *coming* was the fulfillment of that hope. All that the prophets foretold of good was connected with Him, and waited for his arrival. He was 'the High Priest of the good things to come;' He was known for long ages by the name of THE COMING ONE.

Many things forespoken concerning Him seemed inconsistent the one with the other: for He was to die, and yet be the living one; He was to be sorrowful, yet anointed with the oil of gladness; He was to be without form or comeliness, yet also fairer than the children of men; He was to be laid as the burnt offering on the altar, yet He was to sit upon the throne; He was to be poor, yet the riches of both heaven and earth were to be His; He was to be rejected of men, yet He was to be acknowledged as King and Lord; He was to be human, yet He was to be divine.

These apparent contradictions were difficult to reconcile; and men oftentimes wondered as they compared what they saw in Jesus of Nazareth with what the prophets had spoken concerning the glory of Messiah. Men know not how to solve, by human reasoning, the difficulties that were thus raised, or to answer to themselves the question as to the *impossibilities* of which His character, and person and life seem to be made up. The twice-repeated 'How can' of Nicodemus was a true index of the state of the Jewish mind in reference to Jesus of Nazareth. Men looked at Him but as the son of a carpenter, and they asked themselves, if all the great things could be predicted by the prophets fulfilled in him. There were features of resemblance, no doubt, but so many of unlikeness that they stood in doubt; not reassuring themselves with the thought that all Messiah's glories could not unfold at once, and that men knew not now, they should know hereafter.

The 'How can' of Nicodemus has often operated thus in subsequent ages and destroyed faith. Men turn away from difficulties and imagine everything to be a contradiction of which they cannot discover the reconciliation. They take a false view, as well as a false measure of difficulties, and of what they call 'impossibilities.'

The miracles of Jesus were meant to meet the 'How can' of Nicodemus; and this was so far well expressed, when that half-believing disciple said to Him, 'We know thou art a teacher come from God, for no man can do these miracles that thou doest except God be with him.' These miracles were so remarkable, so peculiar, so numerous, and so like what the prophets had led Israel to expect of Messiah, that they at once raised the question with some — may this be Messiah Himself? There are some things which seem to say, It cannot be He; but there are more, which distinctly say it is He. 'Lo, this is our God, we have waited for Him, and He will save us: this is Jehovah; we have waited for Him, we will be glad and rejoice in His salvation' (Isa. 25:9).

The way in which the Lord met the unbelief of Nicodemus is very peculiar, and asks our notice. 'Thou art a teacher come from God,' said the Pharisee. A Teacher! And is that all? A teacher come from God! But is that all? Then thou art far from the kingdom, and canst not enter it. He who enters that kingdom must own my true and divine Messiahship. None can pass into that kingdom, but they who recognize in me the Messiah, the Christ of God. Thou must be born again; for only 'he who believeth that Jesus is THE CHRIST is born again. To call me teacher will avail nothing; you must acknowledge me as the Christ. Only they who do so are sons and heirs; and none save the sons and heirs can obtain the kingdom. 'As many as received Him (as THE CHRIST) to them gave He power to become the sons of God, even to them that believe on His name; who were born (who received their sonship) not of blood (not by natural descent), nor of the will of the flesh (not by any process of human generation), nor of the will of man (not by any human appointment or choice), but of God' (John 1:12,13): for 'that which is born of the flesh is flesh, and that which is born of the Spirit is spirit' (John 3:6). Our reception of Jesus of Nazareth as Messiah is that which constitutes our sonship, and secures our entrance into the kingdom of God.

Everything therefore depends on our having right thoughts of Christ. Many think that faith and unbelief are of no great importance, either for the better or the worse to us; and that our views of Messiah cannot be the turning point of our admission into or exclusion from the kingdom. In the divine estimate, a right faith — that is, a true creed — is beyond all price, both as to its present effects in securing the divine favor now, and as to its final results in providing for us a right to the inheritance hereafter. It is no vain thing to believe aright, whatever men may say. The value which God sets upon recognition of His Christ, in the fullness of that glory which belongs to Him, is to be measured by the infiniteness of the blessing attaching to all those who believe that 'Jesus is the Christ, the Son of the living God.' The completeness of our creed concerning Him and His work, as the Sent of God, the Only begotten of the Father, is a thing of no minor importance. To add to or take from the words written in the Scriptures regarding Messiah is to forfeit our portion in the kingdom and our place in the Lamb's book of life.

The age professes to be going in a quest of faith. What are we to believe? This is the question that is universally put. Yet, with all this, men attach no value to a right faith, nor will admit that God cares more for the man that believes one thing than for him who believes another. Sentimental earnestness, whether philosophical or religious, is the modern substitute for a right creed; and men are allowed to play fast and loose with truth, without being supposed to incur their present spiritual condition, or any displeasure from God Himself.

Now this is precisely the state in which we should expect to find matters had there been no revelation, and had God left man to grope his way darkly to truth without any help, either external or internal, from above. Without a Bible, men would be tossed hither and thither in their opinions; they would naturally be unwilling to be trammeled by a creed; for any such creed would be but the creed of a man. Religious *truth* could not exist, though religious *speculation* might be rife. There could be no *responsibility* attaching to belief, no *sin* in unbelief, and no *danger* in error; for those three things must arise out of an authoritative revelation from Him who alone can proclaim truth as a certainty, and error as a malignant evil.

The poetry, the philosophy, the science of modern times, seem all to have deliberately gone back to some pre-revelation era, and to have taken their stand upon simple paganism, insofar as religious truth is concerned. 'An infant crying for the light' is the accurate symbol of such teachers, furnished by themselves, and indicating that the true light had never come; and that six thousand years God had cruelly kept His creatures in the dark in all things most worthy of knowing — that is the things pertaining to Himself. 'The Christ that is to be' is the modern watchword of expectation, and the hope given by these men of mind, who, believing that the Christ of past ages has proved a failure, have become expectants of another Messiah, who will embody in himself all philosophy, and poetry, and science; just as the still hoped-for Messiah of Israel is to embody all the ambitious dreams of carnal and unbelieving Judaism. Whether this coming Christ of philosophy will reveal Him who is said to be the 'unknown and unknowable,' they do not tell us; for what they seem to desire is not a revelation of Godhead, but a revelation of humanity, and an incarnation of the intellect: so that if there still remains in the human spirit any longing after Him in whom we live, and move, and have our being, that longing must remain unresponded to, and must content itself with re-erecting the old Athenian altar 'to the unknown God.' That which modern intellect hopes and sighs for is not a Christ in whom God becometh man, but a Christ in whom man becometh God.

The coming Christ of philosophy will simply impersonate man's ideal of the good and true: for no water can rise higher than its source. He will put an end to the supernatural and miraculous, for which the Christ of Bethlehem was the witness. He will be the exhibition of natural goodness, natural knowledge, natural benevolence, and natural morality, in opposition to all that is superhuman and divine.

He will be broad enough, and wide enough, and liberal enough to embrace all religions except one — the religion of THE SIN-BEARING CROSS; and, following in the steps of Roman paganism (whose Pantheon opened its gates to every god but to Jehovah and His incarnate Son), will supremely tolerate every religion of earth, save that of Him whom we are still allowed to own and worship as our God and Lord, Jesus the Christ, who died and rose again. Nay, and he will go back to the double lure by which man was first led into apostasy, and pledge himself to fulfill to man the promise which had hitherto so significantly failed, 'Ye shall be gods, knowing good and evil;' and, 'Ye shall not surely die.' The deification of man, and his consequent security against all evil from without or above, and specifically against all penalty for self will and disobedience, will form the sum of the 'great swelling words' with which he whom philosophers call 'Christ that is to be,' but whom Scripture calls 'the Antichrist,' will persuade men to bow down before him, and own as prophet, priest, and king.

The truth which God has embodied in 'the Christ' is not only different in kind from that which is wrapped up in the physical creation, but it differs in the *consequences of* our receiving or rejecting it. Its lofty nature makes it differ; its supreme importance makes it differ; its more direct bearing on the character and worship of God makes it differ; its effects upon our present spiritual wellbeing make it differ. All these necessarily imply a certain amount of responsibility in dealing with higher truth, and a certain amount of danger in defacing, or disparaging, or rejecting it. But there is one special point of difference which is worthy of gravest notice. The rejection of physical truth does not carry with it positive penalty or direct retribution; the rejection of spiritual truth does. This, no doubt, is denied by many; and the two kinds of truth are affirmed to be precisely on the same footing as to *penalty*. Though by some it may be admitted that there is greater loss or injury in refusing the spiritual than in refusing the physical.

Now we admit that this loss or injury arising from ignorance or disbelief or spiritual truth is a real and permanent evil in itself; for to be without the knowledge of the true God (whether from ignorance or rejection) is to be without that which fills the soul, and imparts gladness, and sustains or comforts in weariness and sorrow. Scripture everywhere attests to this: to become 'acquainted with God' is to become possessed of 'good;' to 'delight ourselves in God' is to get the desires of our heart. The true knowledge of the true God is like sunshine to the soul.

But then this is not all, and it is at this point that one of the great controversies of the present day arises. Does the willful exclusion of this knowledge carry with it positive and divine penalties? It is to be visited hereafter with the displeasure of God as *guilt*, which the righteous Judge must deal with at a judgment seat, and to which He must apportion a retribution according to the greatness of its enormity?

If we are to accept even the conclusions of reason, we must say that, seeing is such a great difference between the two kinds of truth, there must be a greater responsibility connected with the treatment of the one than the other; that there is the likelihood of our being far more seriously injured by the rejection of the one than of the other; and that the fact there being no positive or statutory penalty annexed to the disbelief of the physical does by no means lead to the conclusion that there can be no such punishment connected with the disbelief of the spiritual. The far loftier character of the spiritual truth, its far higher importance, its bearing upon the character and honor of God as well as upon the government of the whole universe, its influence for good or ill to millions of God's creatures — these considerations would rather incline us to believe (apart from revelation) that some special notice must be taken of such a rejection in the shape of judicial condemnation, and the infliction of a penalty corresponding to the evil done and the crime committed.

Yet such a conclusion would not have been demonstration. It opens the way for this, by showing its likelihood and its propriety. But it is to the Scriptures themselves that we must go to learn what God thinks of the evil of impugning any part of that truth which He has embodied in THE CHRIST, and revealed for our acceptance. These teach us in all their parts what value God attaches to His truth — to the whole of His truth — and what stress He lays upon our reception of it as the means of blessing to ourselves and of honor to Him as the God of truth; and what displeasure lies on all who turn the truth of God into a lie, or who refuse to recognize it as divine. 'He that believeth on Him is not condemned; but he that believeth not is condemned already, because he hath not believed in the name of the only begotten Son of God' (John 3:18). Here, then, is the turning point, and here is the verdict of the Judge. Here is the line which separates faith from unbelief, on the one side of which there is life, and on the other death. "He that BELIEVETH hath life; and he that BELIEVETH NOT shall not see life' (John 3:36). To get rid of the condemnation by denying the Book in which it is written, as some are trying to do, is only to add guilt to guilt — the guilt of rejecting the whole to the guilt of rejecting each part separately; the crime of flinging away the casket to the crime of trampling on the gem.

Into the question of what the Book reveals concerning future punishment for the rejection of the Christ, we do not here enter. Scripture has spoken plainly and reveals to us the infliction on the unbeliever of that which it calls 'the wrath of God:' the bearing of that which by the sinner calls forth 'the weeping and wailing and gnashing of teeth,' in opposition to the 'songs and everlasting joy' of him who has accepted the divine testimony of the Christ of God. Lazarus in Abraham's bosom, and the rich man in the place of woe (Luke 16:22, 23), may be thought to be but figures in a parable; yet they are figures which express but too plainly and too awfully the coming consolation and the coming sorrow: He that is unjust, let him be unjust still; and he that is filthy, let him be filthy still; and he that is righteous, let him be righteous still; and he that is holy. let him be holy still' (Rev 22:11). That which is to fall upon the sinner must be something like that which fell on the Substitute, and from which the Substitute came to deliver us, by bearing it for us — that something which made His soul exceeding sorrowful, and caused Him to cry out, 'My God, my God, why hast Thou forsaken me?' That something was the *wrath of God.* What that wrath is, eternity will reveal. It is something real, like what Christ endured; not mere negation; not showing itself in placing its objects beyond the possibility of sensation, as must be the case if the theory of annihilation be true. That the Son of God should be incarnate and should suffer anguish to prevent us from being annihilated seem very unlikely, to say the least and that this should be all the curse from which He came to redeem us (Gal. 3:13) by His cross, seems to be trifling with penalty and righteousness. Assuredly punishment has no such negative meaning among men; and the inflictions of law are a mockery, if they mean merely rendering the guilty victims insensible to either pain or pleasure. Sorrow cannot be the wages of sin, if the sentence of the Judge upon the sinner be, 'Thou shall sorrow no more;' and if the recompense of the wicked is to be expressed in the same words as the reward of the righteous, 'The days of thy mourning shall be ended.' To say to the sinner, Thou shalt rejoice no more, may look like penalty, as being the deprivation of the possibility of happiness; but then that sentence that cuts off all sorrow too; so that to all alike the words will equally apply, 'Thou shalt weep no more!'

All that is implied in condemnation for a rejected Christ, I do not undertake to discuss; but it *must* mean more than wiping away all tears form the unbeliever's eyes.

That God should lay such a burden (the burden of our guilt) upon His Son, implied that there was something very awful in store for sinners. If that something was the mere extinction of being, it is difficult to see what the Son of God really bore, or for what He made atonement. Did God's displeasure against the sinning object exhaust itself in the depriving him of existence — in reducing him to nothing? If this is all that is symbolized in the fire of the altar, or implied in that which Scripture calls 'wrath' and 'the curse,' the whole institution of sacrifice is unmeaning, and the cross a mockery — nay, a useless piece of cruelty to One whose innocence deserved far other treatment. Nay, the cross is not only 'made of none effect,' but is really the greatest *injustice* that was perpetrated on earth; an injustice enough in itself to dissolve all law, to make void all equity and fairness, to subvert every idea of divine goodness and love, to efface all distinctions between right and wrong, between the innocent and the guilty. That God should not spare His Son, and yet spare all His rejecters and all impenitents from all the pain flowing from their misdeeds, by extinguishing them forever, seems an unrighteousness amounting to an impossibility.

If it is thought that all offenders should go free, and that the highest kind of criminals (despisers of God and His law) do not deserve punishment at all, let it be said so, and we shall know how to meet the statement; but that men should admit *punishment* to be a right thing, without which the world would go to wreck, and good be confounded with evil, and yet that the Judge's sentence against the very worst will only be, 'Depart, ye cursed, into *everlasting non-suffering*,' would be setting up a throne of iniquity such as no earthly government could tolerate.

If the Christ of God be truly God's beloved Son, worthy of honor and love form all creaturehood, are those who refuse Him this love and honor to incur no guilt, and to suffer no penalty? Is the highest crime in the universe — treason against the King of kings and Lord of lords — to be passed by, or rather rewarded, by consigning the traitor to such a state of eternal unconsciousness that no punishment can be possible; that his earthly miseries shall be ended; and that his own conscience shall never be able to unbraid him for the lifelong crime which he persisted in committing, but which he can afford to laugh at, inasmuch as it merely involved his losing an existence which had become not worth the keeping, and of which, in mercy, the Judge, as a reward for his wickedness, is to deprive him forever!

All this may be benevolence, or good nature, or dislike of inflicting pain, or indifference to evil; but it is not *law*, it is not *righteousness*. And the carrying out of it will turn not this world merely, but the universe, upside down, making the order and happiness of creation an everlasting impossibility; destroying all sense of security to the saved, because proceeding on no principle of rectitude toward the lost. Besides, it would be a poor exhibition even of philanthropy;

for it might justly be said, If divine benevolence can go so far, why can it not go a little further? If it can set aside the infliction of punishment, why should it not abolish or prevent all present suffering as well as all future; nay, why should it not confer happiness? If it finds no law against the former, can it find any law against the latter? Partial philanthropy like this is both weak and unjust. It makes void both law and love. It is unfair alike to the lost and the saved.

This playing fast and loose with law and penalty, with evil and good, with sorrow and joy, is evidently the invention of men, who, fearing the consequences of their own misdeeds, try to persuade themselves that, if the worst comes to the worst, and they are condemned at last, God will extinguish their existence rather than see them suffer. This weak and vacillating philanthropy receives no countenance from the long stern ages of human suffering; and of it there is certainly no indication in the cross of Christ.

CHAPTER 4

PETER'S CONFESSION TO THE CHRIST

It will be well to turn to some of the many declarations or confessions made in the New Testament concerning Jesus of Nazareth as the Christ of God. They embody the faith of the disciples; they proclaim Israel's faith; they exhibit to us the faith on which the Church is built, and on which she has rested, is resting still, and will continue to rest till He comes again. For the creed of the Church is one; and though man has tried to tear it in pieces, or supplant it with beliefs of his own, it remains to the end — one and the same: like Him who is its sum and burden, Jesus Christ, the same yesterday, today, and forever. It is a veritable creed, uttered by an apostle, and sanctioned by the Master Himself. Thus, then, in few words, we read the Church's early creed, given sometimes by one and sometimes by another.

(1) The angel at Bethlehem is the first to give us the 'symbol' (Luke 2:11): 'Unto you is born this day, in the city of David, a SAVIOR, which is CHRIST the LORD.' The Savior, the Christ, the Lord, are the three great words in which it is summed up; each of these contains 'the good tidings of great joy.'

(2) The angel, before His birth, had said, 'Thou shalt call His name JESUS' (Matt. 1:21); Joseph at His birth 'called His name Jesus' (Matt. 1:25); at His circumcision 'His name was called JESUS' (Luke 2:21). Here we have the briefest form of the creed, and yet in this the great essence is retained; for JESUS, that is, Jehovah the Savior,' is really creed.

(3) The next is John the Baptist, who, in the well-known words, 'Behold the Lamb of God, which taketh away the sin of the world' (John 1:29), sums up the whole book of Leviticus, and gives us the essence and meaning of all sacrifice from the beginning.

(4) The fourth is that of Andrew, 'Simon Peter's brother,' and runs in these words: 'We have found THE MESSIAS; which is, being interpreted, the Christ' (John 1:41). Messias! That word was the summing of Israel's creed, and also of ours.

(5) The fifth is Nathanael's: 'Rabbi, Thou art the SON OF GOD, Thou art the KING of Israel' (John 1:49). Here is another article in the old belief; and yet not another, for it was wrapped up in the following. Jesus of Nazareth is the

Son of God, and Israel's King! The knowledge of this is life eternal, for in it is embodied the fullness of the grace of God.

(6) The next is Peter's (Matt. 16:16; Mark 8:29; Luke 9:20). Putting together the words as given by all the evangelists, the confession runs thus: 'THOU art THE CHRIST…the CHRIST OF GOD.' 'Thou art the CHRIST, the Son of the living God.' Thus we get piece after piece of the wondrous creed, and each succeeding fragment or article brings out more fully 'the love of God which is in Christ Jesus our Lord.'

(7) The next is Martha's: 'I believe that Thou art THE CHRIST, the Son of God, which should come into the world.'[1] (John 11:27). This was the summing up of her creed; it was the beginning and end both of her faith and hope. To know Jesus as the Christ, the Son of God, was to have everlasting life, and to be an heir of the kingdom. In the Old Testament Scriptures she had the whole revelation of God as to Messiah and Messiah's work, and all this she now connected with Him whom she knew by the name of Jesus; and in Him she saw the embodiment of all that the fathers had been looking for.

(8) The next is that of Thomas: 'My Lord and my God' (John 20:28), — carrying us back to Isa.25.9: 'Lo, this is *our God*; we have waited for Him: this is *the Lord* (Jehovah); we have waited for Him.' For it was a *divine* Messiah that Israel had

been looking for; and it is such that Thomas now sees, and hears, and touches.

All these confessions are thus summed up by the Apostle John, towards the close of his Gospel, and connected with THE LIFE which Messiah came to bring. 'Many other signs truly did Jesus in the presence of His disciples, which are not written in this book: but these are written, that ye might believe that JESUS IS THE CHRIST, THE SON OF GOD; and that believing ye might have life through His name' (John 20:30). We find this form of words more than made use of by the Apostle John: 'Whosoever believeth that Jesus is the Christ is born of God' (1 John 5:1); connecting belief in Jesus as the Christ with sonship, and taking us back to John 1:12 and 3:1-8. Thus life, and sonship, and heirship, as well as pardon and deliverance, are connected with believing in Jesus as the Christ. For these words are divine and living, conveying to him who receives them the blessing which they contain. 'The words that I speak unto you, they are spirit, and they are life' (John 6:63). The abiding of Christ's *words* in us is always associated with the abiding of *life*, with the presence of Him of whom they speak, and with overwhelming the world[2] (1 John 5:4): 'Whosoever shall confess that Jesus is the Son of God, God dwelleth in him, and he in God' (1 John 4:15). Nay more, they are associated with the indwelling of that *love* which they reveal: 'We have known and believed the love that God hath to us.

God is love; and he that dwelleth in love dwelleth in God, and God in him.'

It will be well, however, to select one of these confessions; not indeed omitting the others, but noticing especially some of the circumstances in which it was uttered. Let us take up that of Peter, as given by three of the evangelists, with slight variations — variations which help to bring out in diverse aspects the whole truth. For all such differences are accredited by the Spirit, or rather, they are expressly framed by the Spirit, in order to bring out all sides of the great confession on which rests the Church of God, and out of which spring the various doctrines which have made up her one creed; her creed concerning the true God and His Son Jesus Christ. The first promise regarding the woman's seed was very brief; yet it contained the sum of divine truth on which the patriarchs lived and died. It afterwards was explained in broader terms, and the Old Testament being that expansion of that promise. Now again, at the commencement of a new era, the creed contracts itself to a single article, substantially the same as that out of which all previous expansions had come; and Messiah Himself gives sanction to this brief confession, as containing the sum of saving knowledge: 'Thou art the Christ' (Mark 8:29).

It will be interesting to notice in detail the circumstances connected with this confession of Peter. We shall find completely everything in the scene is linked with Him who is the subject of the confession. Here, as elsewhere, Christ is 'all, and in all.' Of the group He is the center; of speakers He is the chief. Our eyes do not fasten themselves on the disciple who makes the confession, but on the Master who drew it forth. His attractions eclipse all others; and here, as on the Transfiguration Mount, we behold no one save 'Jesus only;' we hear no one save 'Jesus only.'

It is a *wayside* conversation that the evangelists record between the Lord and His disciples. Yet were not these disciples 'wayside heators' in the sense of the parable. It was on good ground that the seed was sown. They were going northward, from Bethsaida to Caesarea Philippi, along the margin of the waters of Merom, the most sequestered, and amongst the most beautiful, of many fair scenes of Palestine. By the way, He spoke to them, and they to Him. The theme was Himself, and He was at once the Teacher and the Lesson. It was on the extreme north of Palestine that the conversation took place, in the locality out of which sprang the well-known description of the land, 'from *Dan* to Beersheba.' Far from Jerusalem and its temple, far from the distinguished cities either of the Old Testament or of the New, was this wondrous confession spoken. Not to a crowd, not in the midst of scribes and Pharisees, or of publicans and sinners but simply to the twelve, was it given. The great seed was to be deposited first in their hearts, as they walked quietly along the lakeside, with mountains on either side, Lebanon full in view, and Hermon in front, with its sparkling snows.

It was just before the transfiguration, as if He would prepare them for that scene, and draw out of them their thoughts concerning

Him, before showing Himself to them in His glory. Ere He leads them up the mountain, He wished them to realize who He really was, that they might recognize in the transfiguration-glory the glory of THE CHRIST, of Israel's Messiah, the Son of God.

It was Peter who made the confession, but he made it in the name of all the disciples. He speaks, and they add their Amen to what is spoken. They might not fully understand all that the name implied, 'the Christ;' but they knew what the prophets from the beginning had spoken, and they knew what the nation believed concerning Messiah, and their confession was not made in ignorance and blindness. Yet scarcely had this confession been made than 'Peter *took* Him' (laid hold of Him), 'and began to *rebuke* Him' (Mark 8:32). What! Rebuke Him whom he had acknowledged to be 'the Christ, the Son of God'? We know not in what language to describe or to condemn such conduct. Yet, strange, notwithstanding this, the Lord selects Peter as one of the favored three who were to stand on the 'holy mount' along with Moses and Elias. Surely here, as elsewhere, 'the grace of our Lord was exceeding abundant' (1 Tim. 1:14); and surely here Jesus Christ 'shows forth all long-suffering, for a pattern to them who should hereafter believe on Him to life everlasting' (1 Tim. 1:16).

It was of 'Jesus of Nazareth' that the confession was made; of Him who had grown up among them as a tender plant, and as a root out of a dry ground. They knew Him as the son of the carpenter, the brother of some Galilean fisherman, the native of a city whose name was a byword; yet they own Him as the Christ. They had hitherto acknowledged Him as the son of Mary, of the seed of Abraham, of the family of David; now they avow their belief in Him as the Christ, the Son of the living God.

It was to Him that the confession was made. They avow their faith in His Messiahship to Himself, that He may hear it and sanction it as a true belief, no cunningly devised fable, nor dream of their own enthusiasm. It is as if, before proclaiming it to the world, they fell down before Him and owned His Christhood. They do not merely whisper to one another, or say to themselves in secret — surely our Master is the Christ. They kneel before Him in reverence, and say, face to face, as if asking His approval, 'Thou art the Christ;' thus making the declaration doubly sure — His own as well as theirs. They say, "Thou art the Christ;' He answers, 'I am.' They confess Him to Himself before they are allowed to confess Him before men.

It was in reply to two questions of His own that this avowal of faith was made. The first was, 'Whom do men say that I am?' and the second, 'Whom say YE that I am?' He first inquires into the world's faith, that He may bring out the prevailing ignorance and error; and then He probes and tests the disciples, in order to draw out the difference between them and the men around. Thus He draws out the faith of His own that He may stamp it with His own mark; just as, on another occasion, He put the question to the Jews, 'What think ye of Christ?' (or, 'What is your judgment concerning the Christ?') in order to bring forth their views, whether of faith or unbelief; and still He asks the same questions of us, 'What think YE of Christ?' and 'Whom say YE that I am?' For He knows how much depends on the right answer to such questions. It is no neither idle nor random inquiry that He makes, but momentous beyond measure, as involving, in the answer to it, eternal consequences; nay, as involving in it its right solution the whole matter of our relationship to God. For if he that believeth that Jesus is the Christ is born of God, and hath everlasting life, then he who does not believe that Jesus is the Christ is not born of God hath not life eternal.

The name of *Christ*, or *Messiah*, had a special meaning to a Jew. It went back over the whole history of the land, the nation, the race. It embodied all its hopes. It gathered up into itself all the promises, and prophecies, and types, and symbols. It carried him back to David, to Moses, to Abraham, to Adam. It called up not only Jerusalem and Bethlehem, but Paradise; for it was linked inseparably with the first promise, as well as with the first altar and the first sacrifice. For we cannot separate the promise from the sacrifice, nor the sacrifice from the promise. Each without the other is dark. The promise alone is a riddle without a key to it; and the sacrifice alone is a key without a riddle.

No doubt Israel's blindness was great; and even the disciples were slow of heart to believe all that the prophets had spoken (Luke 24:25).[3] But still they knew enough of the prophets to understand much of what and who *the Christ* was to be; and in speaking of Him, they spoke of One in whom they saw not only the superhuman, but the divine — a divine Deliver and King — one who was coming as the messenger of love, not to Israel only, but to man, and the man's earth. They could not at this time comprehend such words as, 'Ye know the grace of our Lord Jesus Christ, that though He was rich, for your sakes He become poor, that ye by His poverty might be rich' (2 Cor. 8:9); but they gathered this at least concerning Messiah from the promise and the sacrifice, that He was God Himself, coming to sinners on an errand of grace, and that in that grace, law was to be honored, and righteousness to be exalted. For the name of Messiah had all along been associated as distinctly with righteousness as with love.

CHAPTER 5

THOU ART THE CHRIST. WHAT THEN?

Let us suppose the Master's question put to us in these days by the Master Himself, as of old.

What would be our answer? What should we say to Him, or to ourselves, or to the Church, or to the world?

We might say, 'Thou art the Christ;' but how much would that express?

With many it would express much less than Peter meant: for Peter, as one versed on the old revelation, knew much that many, calling themselves Christians, are ignorant of. With many, however, it would express more than Peter could have implied; for 'the darkness is past, and the true light now shineth.' They have seen what Peter had not then seen: the cross, the grave, and the resurrection. The light from the cross has wonderfully illuminated that name, THE CHRIST. It was but dim to Peter; it is bright to us.

'Thou art the Christ,' we say. If so, what do we mean, and what follows from that meaning?

What do we mean? We know what a true Israelite would mean; and our meaning, though much fuller, must be substantially the same. If Thou art the Christ, then,

1. Thou art the Seed of the Woman.

Thou art He in whom God's first great promise to man finds its fulfillment: true seed of the *woman*. Thou art the Life, because of whom she was called *Eve*, the Life — true Son of Adam, very man, Thyself 'the last Adam' (1 Cor. 15:45), 'the second man, the Lord from heaven' (I Cor. 15:47). Thou art He to whom the eyes of our first parents were turned, and in whom they rested, though to them Thou wert the *promise*d seed, the Coming One. For it was through man that God was to save man; and as by one *man's* disobedience many had been made sinners, so by one *man's* obedience many were to be made righteous. Through her who had been 'beguiled' (2 Cor. 11:3), through her who 'was deceived' and 'was in the transgression' (1 Tim. 2:13, 14), was the great Deliver to come: very man — made of a woman, bone of our bone, and flesh of our flesh. He was more truly man than the fallen sons of Adam, for sin did not belong to humanity at first, and He was without sin: the holy seed, the holy child.

Thus we have in Christ a child of time, yet a child of eternity. He was born of a woman, yet He is from everlasting to everlasting God. The first thing we read of Him as a son of Eve is in these words regarding His mother, 'She was found with child of the Holy Ghost' (Matt. 1:18); and again, 'That which is conceived in her is of the Holy Ghost' (Matt 1:20). Ages before, this song had been sung:

Behold!
The Virgin shall conceive,
And bear a son;
And shall call His name Immanuel (Isa. 7:14).

And another song had been sung, very like the former, yet fuller and more exultant:

Unto us the child is born,
Unto us the son is given;
And the government shall be upon His shoulders,
And His name shall be called
Wonderful,
Counsellor,
The Mighty God,
The Everlasting Father,
The Prince of Peace (Isa. 9:6).

And then, just before the birth of this seed of the woman, the angel Gabriel comes to His Mother with these words:

Fear not, Mary,
For thou hast found favor with God.
Behold! Thou shalt conceive in thy womb,
And bring forth a son,
And thou shall call His name Jesus

The Holy Ghost shall come upon thee,
And the power of the Highest shall overshadow thee:
Therefore also that holy thing,
Shall be called
The Son of God (Luke 1:30, 35).

Then we come to the actual birth of the predicted seed: 'She brought forth her firstborn son, and wrapped Him in swaddling-clothes, and laid Him in a manger' (Luke 2:7). On this we hear the glorious message from above:

Fear not!
Behold!
I bring you good tidings of great joy,
Which shall be to all people,
For unto you is born this day,

In the city of David, a Savior,
Who is Christ the Lord (Luke 2:11).

Thus we are brought first to Jerusalem, for there Isaiah's prediction was uttered; then to Nazareth, for there the annunciation was given; and lastly to Bethlehem, where the child was born. What a history is contained in the manger-cradle of that child, and what a revelation of the invisible God! O child of Bethlehem, what a story had been Thine, and what a story is yet to be Thine! For the history of the universe, past, present, and to come revolves round Thee. O seed of the woman, what a manifestation of Godhead is given to us in Thee! On Thy stony cradle is written, GOD IS LOVE. On the gate of the city where Thou wast born is inscribed, GOD IS LOVE. On Thy tomb after years was graven, GOD IS LOVE. And on that throne where now Thou art seated is engraved, GOD IS LOVE.

Yes Thou art the Christ, the Son of God, the Savior of the world; Thy name is Jesus, and it is also Immanuel. We look to Thee and live. We look into Thy cradle, and are comforted. Thou art bone of our bone, and flesh of our flesh; 'Christ is all, and in all.' Though rich, for our sakes Thou becamest poor, that we by poverty might be rich. We have nothing to give Thee, but Thou hast everything to give us; and we are content to be simple receivers of Thy liberality and fullness.

2. *Thou art the Son of the Living God.*

Thou art the eternal Son, who couldest say, 'I and my Father are one' (John 10:30). Thou art very man, yet also very God; all Godhead and all mankind in Thy person; the everlasting link between heaven and earth, between Creator and creature; God manifest in flesh; heir of all things; God over all, blessed forever; Thy name Jehovah, and Thy glory divine. Now then we know all that man can do for us, and that God can do for us here. All heaven is here, all earth is here. God Himself had taken the side of man; yea, has become man, that He may accomplish man's deliverance. The incarnation is certainly not the whole of the mighty undertaking. It is but the beginning. Yet it is a wondrous pledge of love. He who came, on man's account, from the throne of God to the manager of Bethlehem, must love man with no common love. He cannot have ceased to care for earth; He cannot have had His love quenched by rebellion, nor turned into coldness by the unworthiness and unlovableness of its objects.

Here, then, we learn at Bethlehem that *God is love*: for it is God whom we see in the manger. We hear that a child has been born. We come to its cradle, and we find God is there. It is 'the Word made flesh' that lies there. The brightness of Jehovah's glory and the express image of His person are there. That cradle gives us God's thoughts of God — what God wishes us to know and think about Him. It shows us how accessible God is, and how He wishes to be approached by us. It shows us how near He has come to us, how low

He has stooped, how truly one with us He has become. It is God — the Son of the living God — very God, who lies there. We see but helpless infancy; yet the mighty power of God is there. We see but clouds and shadows resting over us; yet on His forehead is written, 'God is light, and in Him is no darkness at all.' The more that we can realize of God in connection with that babe and that cradle, the more we shall know of Him who said, 'My thoughts are not your thoughts.' Here God speaks to us, and we to Him. These little fingers are those of Him who ere longed to touch the sick, and to heal them with His power. These hands are the hands which are soon to be pierced with nails. That head is soon to be crowned with thorns. These feet are to be fastened to the cross. These eyes are to weep at the grave of Lazarus and over Jerusalem. That body which now lies in a stony cradle is soon to lie in a stony tomb. And yet all these things link themselves with His Godhead. The Son of the living God is here; and Jesus of Nazareth is He — the very Christ of God.

3. *Thou art the Angel of the Covenant.*

Thy name is 'the Angel of the Lord,' or the 'Angel Jehovah' (Gen 16:7, 13, 18:1, 2, 17, 48:16; Judg. 6:11-24), or the Angel of Covenant (Mal. 3:7). Thou art He to whom the name Jehovah appertains; Jehovah, and Jehovah's Messenger; the *Sent* of the Father (John 6:44), His true Siloam (John 9:7), His covenant Angel, to do His redeeming work on earth among the sons of men.

All Israel's history is full of this Angel and His doings; every Jew knew His name in connection with God's interpositions of grace and power; every Jew connected that mysterious messenger with Messiah. Angel He was, yet more than angel in the excellency of His power and in the greatness of His love. 'The Angel of His presence saved them' (Isa. 63:9) is the story of many a chapter in Israel's annals. Oftentimes, when things were at their worst, out from the Lord this Angel came and wrought salvation by His mighty power. 'The arm of the Lord awoke, and put on strength;' and Israel recognized in this the interposition of their own Messiah, of Him who was afflicted in all their affliction, who had again and again said, How shall I give thee up, O Israel? How shall I deliver thee up, O Ephraim? — of Him who, looking back upon His own gracious dealings with the ever-murmuring, ever-rebelling nation in ages past, uttered these words of love — perhaps the warmest, truest, tenderest words of love ever breathed from human lips: 'O Jerusalem, Jerusalem, how often would I have gathered thy children as a hen doth gather her chickens under her wings; and ye would not! Yes, and while uttering these words of love, the Angel of the Covenant wept — wept because they would not be saved, because they would not be blest! 'Not willing that any should perish, but that all should come to repentance' had been Messiah's feeling towards them on all their apostasies; and in that coming day, when we shall get behind the outward into the inward, and see the true interior of Christ's dealings with men, and the unseen beatings of His gracious heart toward the chief of sinners, who are repelling all His advances, we shall know how sincere His long-suffering had been, how profound His pity, how earnest His proposals of reconciliation, how tender His yearnings, how honest His tears over the rejectors of His love.

God's eternal purpose shall stand; His election, according to the good pleasure of His will, shall be carried out; but not the less shall it be found true, that the wings extended by Messiah over Jerusalem, under which He would fain have gathered her children, were the wings of truest tenderness as well as of almighty power. The day for the reconciliation of these apparent difficulties will come, and we shall know the harmony between the purpose and the love.

4. *Thou art the great Sacrifice.*

In Thee all sacrifice centers; from Thee the four great offerings spring, and into Thee they return. Thou art also the burnt offering, the peace offering, the trespass offering, the sin offering, all in one. Thou art also the meat offering and the drink offering. In Thee we see the double offering of the day of atonement, and the paschal lamb with its unleavened bread. In each of these we discern some special feature of Thy work for sinners, and some peculiar characteristic of Thy person as the sin bearer. Yes, if Jesus of Nazareth be the Christ of God, then He is the propitiation for our sins — the Lamb of God which taketh away the sin of the world. Of Him the book of Leviticus is full.

Of Him the whole tabernacle speaks — especially the altar, and the laver, and the mercy seat. There Christ is all, and in all; and every vessel there Christ is all, and in all; every vessel there points to His sin-bearing work. It is the tabernacle of the Substitute; for take away the idea of substitution, and the tabernacle, with its varied furniture and sacrifices, is an unmeaning fabric — a mere national tent, round which the people gather, and where the tribes celebrate some unmeaning rites, as useless as those of the heathen around. The complete bearing of sin by another; one life for another; the just for the unjust: this is the great truth embodied in the tabernacle. Substitution, ransom, sacrifice, propitiation, atonement, suretyship: these are words whose meaning comes fully out in connection with the tabernacle and its services. They are inscribed on every vessel and every curtain; they speak out in every ceremony, and in every victim, in every priest and Levite. The fire, the smoke, the incense, and the blood, declare the truth contained in these words beyond mistake or doubt.

The Psalms, too — at least such as the twenty-second, the fortieth, the sixty-ninth, and eighty-eighth — unfold the sufferings of the Substitute when bearing our sins; as when He says, 'My God, my God, why hast Thou forsaken me?' (Ps. 22:1); and, 'The wrath lieth hard upon me, Thou hast afflicted me with all Thy waves...I am afflicted, and ready to die from my youth up' (Ps 88:7, 15). And then the fifty-third of Isaiah gives the key both to the book of Leviticus and Psalms: 'He is despised and rejected of men; a man of *sorrows*, and acquainted with *grief*...Surely He hath borne OUR *griefs*, and carried OUR *sorrows*. He was wounded for Our transgressions; He was bruised for Our iniquities.'

In connection with all these, we hear the cry on the cross, 'It is finished!' We see the veil rent in twain, and we learn that 'this man, after He had offered one sacrifice for sins forever, sat down on the right hand of God' (Heb. 10:12). Now, then, there remaineth no more conscience of sins (Heb. 10:1) to them that receive the divine testimony to the finished sacrifice. In believing the record, they obtain the forgiveness and the 'no condemnation' which come through Him who was 'delivered for our offenses, and raised again for our justification.' O perfect sacrifice, what is there that a sinner, burdened with guilt and weary of the evil within him, does not find in Thee? He finds peace for trouble, liberty for bondage, righteousness for unrighteousness, fullness for emptiness, holiness for pollution, rest for weariness, light for darkness, life for death — all, all in Thee!

5. *Thou art the Prophet like unto Moses.*

Yes, Thou art a Prophet, yet more than a prophet; like unto Moses, yet greater than Moses; the world's true Teacher, both in things past and in things to come: a Prophet such as earth has never seen, 'in whom are hid all the treasures of wisdom and knowledge' (Col. 2:3). Earth needs a prophet, and Thou art He! Man should fain be his own prophet, but he prophesies only folly and deceit. Thou only art what so many among us call 'the Prophet of humanity.' Thou art not 'a teacher come from God,' as Nicodemus called Thee, but THE TEACHER, the one Teacher of Israel and the Church; the only Teacher who could ever say, "I AM the Truth.'

Yes, in these last days we need a teacher, more than ever: a divine and perfect teacher, in whose skill and instruction we can have fullest confidence, and in whose love we can entirely rest. He who taught the multitude in the days of His flesh is the teacher for us. He who never made one mistake in His teaching; who never refused to teach even the dullest; who never lost His temper with the most forward of His scholars; who never grudged His time and trouble to anyone; who never exercised any needless or untender discipline; who was Father, Brother, Teacher, all in one — this Teacher is ours.

It is He, the Prophet like unto Moses, that says, 'Give ear, O ye heavens, and I will speak; and hear, O earth, the words of my mouth. My doctrine shall drop as the rain, my speech shall distil as the dew' (Deut. 32:1). All that was in Moses is in Him. All Samuel and David, all Isaiah, and Jeremiah, Ezekiel, Daniel, and Elijah and Elisha, we find in Him; nothing lacking, and nothing unreal, nothing exaggerated, but all wisdom, and earnestness, and gentleness, and calmness. Just such a prophet as we need is He, this Jesus of Nazareth, this Christ of God.

To each of us, with the true voice of a teacher, 'who had compassion on the ignorant,' He says, 'Learn of me.' He advises for pupils; He entreats us to be scholars in His school, to become 'disciples,' and to hear the words of His lips. The gate of His school is ever open, and He gives His instructions freely. All are welcome! Doth He not cry? Doth He not put forth His voice? Doth He not say, 'O ye simple, understand wisdom; and ye fools, be of an understanding heart. Hear, for I will speak of excellent things; and the opening of my lips shall be right things. For my mouth shall speak truth...Receive my instruction, and not silver; and knowledge rather than choice gold' (Pro. 8:1-10). Yet this unteachable world refuses to learn, preferring every other prophet to Him, and every other instruction to His; loving the darkness rather than the light, and preferring error to truth.

6. Thou art the Anointed One.

The true anointing is with Thee, and in Thee; the fullness of the Spirit dwells in Thee, and the divine unction rests upon Thee; for the Father 'giveth not the Spirit by measure unto Thee' (John 3:34). This anointing is that from which Messiah takes His name. He is the Messiah, the Christ, because of the anointing, because of His being filled with the Spirit. 'The Spirit of the Lord God is upon me, because the Lord hath anointed me' (Isa. 61:1); and because of this, He is once and again spoken of us as 'the Anointed One' (Ps. 2:2). He is anointed as the Prophet, as the Priest, as the King, anointed not only with the Spirit of power and wisdom, but 'with the oil of gladness above His fellows' (Ps. 45:7). This anointing is for us. He received it that He might preach the gospel, 'good tidings to the meek' (Isa. 61:1); that He might bind up the broken-hearted; that He might give beauty for ashes, the oil of joy for mourning. And now that He has been glorified, He dispenses this Spirit in His fullness, as at Pentecost. Having received gifts for men, even for the rebellious, He distributes these gifts to His Church with open heart and hand, so that she has all and abounds. And if she in our day exhibits only leanness, it is because she puts away the fullness which He, as 'the Christ,' presents to her from His heavenly throne. Open thy mouth wide, and I will fill it,' He says to her.

Why, then, should the Church be poor, so long as her Head is rich? Why should any saint be empty, so long as Christ is full? Why should any of earth's rebellious ones refuse to come and partake of the divine fullness of the Spirit, so freely held out to the needy sons of men?[2] Here are some of the unsearchable riches of the Christ set before us. They come down on us abundantly, overflowing out of His fullness; and we have but to let them be poured into our lap.

7. *Thou art Jehovah-Tsidkenu, the Lord our Righteous* (Jer.23:6).

Thou hast given of righteousness for our life of unrighteousness; a life obedience for our life of disobedience. Thy perfection covers our imperfection in every part: Thou art our righteousness; Thou art the righteousness of God for us; Thou art made unto us righteousness; Thou, who knewest no sin, wast made sin for us, that we might be made the righteousness of God in Thee. We put Thee on — Thee, the righteous One; Thou art 'the best robe,' the robe which the Father hath provided for us; Thou art the 'garment of salvation,' and the 'robe of righteousness' (Isa. 61:10); so that, when arrayed in these, it is said to each of us, Thou art perfect through the comeliness which I have put upon thee' (Ezek. 16:14).

Messiah then, in the divine purpose, was to be the 'righteousness of God' for us. Not only does He make us righteousness by His power, but He is our righteousness — the righteousness which God has provided — the righteousness of the incarnate Godhead. 'Their righteousness is of me, saith the Lord' (Isa. 54:17).

The righteousness of God, simply as God, was not enough for us, nay was not suitable; the righteousness of man, as man, was wholly insufficient. But the righteousness of Him who was both God and man, who had all divine and all human righteousness was just what we needed. They who affirm that the righteousness of God of which the apostle speaks (Rom. 3:21) means merely the divine attribute or perfection known by that name, overthrow redemption; not only do they destroy the apostle's argument in that epistle, but subvert totally the justification of the sinner as provided by God in Christ Jesus. For 'Christ is the end of the law for RIGHTEOUSNESS to everyone that believeth' (Rom. 10:4); that is, He has fulfilled the law, in order to provide a RIGHTEOUSNESS by which the sinner is justified in believing. For in believing we receive 'the righteousness;' in believing we are 'justified;' in believing we are so placed in oneness with Him who is the Lord our righteousness, that we are henceforth treated by God as if *we* had lived the righteous life that He lived, as if *we* had done all the righteous things which He did, and spoke all the righteous words which He spoke. Though still sinners, and deeply conscience of evil, we know that in our righteous Representative we are reckoned righteous, and dealt with by God as if all our unrighteousness had never been, nay as if we had done the righteousness which He has done as our surety and our substitute. Recognizing His vicarious life and death as that on which we stand before God, and shall hereafter take our stand before the judgment seat, we realize the truth, 'As He is, so are we in this world' (I John 4:17). 'The Lord is well pleased for His righteousness' sake' (Isa. 42:21); so well pleased *with Him*, and with what He has done, and so well pleased *because* of Him, and because of what He has done, that He causes His well-pleasedness to rest on everyone who accepts His testimony to the Beloved Son.

It is the judge Himself who proposed the plan of acquittal and provided the substitute. We fall in with His plan, we accept the substitute, and are thus put in possession of the righteousness. With the Judge upon our side, we have nothing to fear; and we know that He is upon the side of all who are willing to own their condemnation and accept His substitute.[3]

8. *Thou art the Light of the World.*

LIGHT has always been associated with Messiah; and every Jew would remember this. As we read the prophets, we find this written everywhere; and looking into the face of Jesus of Nazareth, we say, Thou art the light, set for the enlightening of every man, the Sun of a dark world. Thou art He by whom the long darkness is to be banished, and the world made what is was originally designed to be — a world of light. Thou, O Jesus, art earth's true light, man's true light!

The veil had been spread over all nations, and Messiah came to remove it; the light for ages shone in the darkness, though the darkness did not receive it. Ages before He came, He was announced as the Star out of Jacob (Num. 24:17), as the Sun of righteousness (Mal. 4:2). The light that Israel had in their dwellings was light from Him (Ex. 10:23). His was the light that beamed out of the pillar cloud. (Ex. 14:20). His was the 'light of the morning' predicted by David (2 Sam. 23:4). His was the light of which we read so often in the Psalms, 'The Lord is my light' (Ps. 27:1). His is the light that is 'sown for the righteous' (Ps. 97:11). It is He whom Isaiah calls the 'light of Israel' (10:17); and of whom he says to Israel, 'Arise, shine, for thy light is come' (60:1); and 'the Lord shall be thine everlasting light' (60:1). He was the dayspring from on high (Luke 1:78), the light to lighten the Gentiles (Luke 2:32); and it is of Him that the evangelist wrote, 'In Him was life, and THE LIFE was the LIGHT of men' (John 1:4). He himself took up the ancient symbol and applied it to Himself, 'I am THE LIGHT of the world' ((John 8:12, 7:5).

As the revealer of the Father, He is the light of the world; as the forgiver of sin, He is the light of the world; as the raiser of the dead, He is the light of the world. Already in some measure this has been exhibited; but when He comes the second time, it shall be more fully seen how truly He is the 'day star' (2Pet. 1:19). He is the bright and morning star (Rev. 2:28, 22:16). All light is in Him; the light of the knowledge of the glory of God is in the face of Jesus Christ (2 Cor. 4:6). We look to Him and are lightened (Ps. 34:5). That which we see in Him gives us light; for in Him is no darkness at all. All the gracious character of God is exhibited in Him, the man Christ Jesus; and he that seen Him hath seen the Father. In believing on Him, we pass through darkness into light; and in continuing to believe, we continue to enjoy the light. Let us hear the words spoken to the Ephesian Church, 'Awake, thou that sleepest, and arise from the dead, and Christ shall give thee light' (Eph. 5:14). Thus shall we walk as children of the light and of the day, walking in His light, and not in the light of man.

9. Thou art the Shepherd of Israel.

Well has the Holy Spirit chosen this name for Messiah, in reference to the errand of grace on which He has come to earth; and very fully did the Lord Jesus recognize this when He was here, again and again making use of the figure as applicable to Himself and His work.

For feeding and watching his flock, a shepherd needs many qualities. He must not be merely 'a hireling, caring not for the sheep;' but he must love his flock. He must be *tender* in his dealings with them — with the young, and the sickly, and the wandering. He must be *brave*, not dreading danger, not fleeing from the lion and the bear. He must be *strong*, capable of much endurance and labour, able to go far in his quest of his stray ones, to lay hold on them, to lift them to his shoulder, and carry them home. He must be *patient*, not getting angry at their stupidity, or vagrancy, or perverseness; but ever bearing with them, and all the more because of their forwardness. He must be *gentle,* not speaking roughly, nor threatening, nor using harsh measures with them. He must be *watchful*, very watchful, with his eye upon them all, in rain, or wind, or storm, or snow, with little time for rest to himself, content to snatch repose now and then as it may be offered. He must be skillful — skillful in guiding; knowing the country well through which his flock is passing, whether it be desert or good pasture; knowing also the wells and springs by the way, the still waters and the green pastures, the shades whether of rock or groove where they may rest at noon. He must be a *physician* too, able to bind up that which is broken, and to heal that which is sick; to know well where the herbs grow for medicine, or to bind up sores and wounds.

Looking then, up to Jesus of Nazareth, as He asks us, Whom say ye that I am? we answer: Thou art Israel's Shepherd, the Church's Shepherd, and our Shepherd, so that we shall not want. Thou leadest us by the green pastures and the still waters; Thou dost not over-drive one sheep or lamb in all Thy scattered flock; Thou seekest and searchest them out in all places where they are scattered in the cloudy and dark day; Thou seekest that which is lost; Thou bringest again that which is driven away, and bindest up that which is broken, and strengthenest that which is sick; Thou feedest Thy flock like a shepherd; Thou gatherest the lambs with Thy arm, and carriest them in Thy bosom, and greatly leadest those that are with young. Thy sheep hear Thy voice; Thou callest them by name, and leadest them out; Thou goest before them, and they follow thee, for they know Thy voice. Thou art the 'chief Shepherd' (1 Pet. 5:4), the 'great Shepherd' (Heb. 13:20), the 'good Shepherd,' who gavest Thy life for the sheep (John 10:11); and to Thee we say, Give ear, O Shepherd of Israel! Thou that leadest Joseph like a flock, Thou that dwellest between the cherubim, shine forth. Thou art gentle, and tender, and gracious; Thou art strong, and brave, and patient; Thou art watchful and skillful, alike for guidance and for health — Lord Jesus Christ, we look up to Thee! Save, and guide, and protect, and bless, that no evil and no enemy may prevail, but only good come nigh to us.

10. *Thou art the Life of the World.*

Life and light are twins. They are like double stars, separate, yet linked together. He who has the life has the light, and he who has the light has the life. The living One is the light-giving One. But the life of the Christ is a life which, alike in nature, and in power, and in immensity, is like no other life. Let us look at it. Death has spread itself over the earth since the time that man sinned and brought upon himself the doom declared at first by God, 'In a day thou eatest thereof thou shalt surely DIE' (Gen 2:17). Nor is it one kind of death that has come to our race, but death in every form and of every kind has come. That which God calls DEATH has become the heritage of the sons of Adam; and a sore heritage it has been, including in it condemnation, darkness, alienation from God, pain, sorrow, terror, with the separation of the body from the soul, the corruption of the grave, and the second death beyond. Who shall undo all this evil-doing? What second man shall destroy the first death, and cancel the second, with all their temporal and eternal accompaniments? Only He who is preeminently, THE MAN, made of a woman, yet one with the living God. For in order to have death removed, not only in man, or beast, or herb, we must go back to the original fountainhead of being, to Him who not only *has* life but *is* life, and from whom the exuberant overflow of life is sufficient to undo all death, and to impart a life that shall never succumb to the power of death, or of him who has the power of death, again.

Messiah comes! He comes as life; at once the possessor and bestower of life to all who need it. Life to the dead, and life from the dead, is that which the Christ of God proclaims! This is His errand and His work. 'I am come that they might have life, and that they might have it more abundantly' (John 10:10).

Yet He does not give life by a mere command, as at the first creation. There is a hindrance; something has come in along with man's sin, which says that the old way of imparting life is at an end, and that a mere command would be unavailing; for that which has now come in, and exercises sway, is too powerful to be thus dealt with, for it wields the power of law and righteousness. These must be dealt with and pacified ere life can find its way to the dead; for the death was a righteous death, and only by righteousness can it be cancelled.

THE LIFE, then, has come; but it has come to die! Without this *death* of 'the Life,' the quickening voice cannot reach the tomb. 'That which thou sowest is not quickened except it die' (1 Cor. 15:36); 'Except a corn of wheat fall into the ground, and die, it abideth alone: but if it die, it bringeth forth much fruit' (John 12:24). It is the death of 'the Life' that brings life to the dead. Thus it is, that while first Adam was made a living soul, the last Adam was made a quickening spirit (1 Cor. 15:45). The Christ possesses the fullness of life in Himself (John 5:26), but it cannot flow out to us until He dies. He lays down His life, and the life bursts forth over earth: the dying has unbarred the gate, and that gate cannot again be closed.

This is the flesh which has been given for the life of the world, and the blood which has been shed for its thirst.

Thou, O Christ, art our life. Law giveth no life, power imparteth no life, but Thou givest it by Thy death. Thy death has given Thee the power of communicating life. And now each of us may have it freely — the judicial life, which springs out of the 'no condemnation;' and the spiritual life, which is the new creation, the being begotten again. Thou, O Jesus of Nazareth, art truly the Life of the world; Thou hast life enough and love enough for us. And these are not merchandise, to be bought and sold; they are to be had for the taking: for Thou openest Thy hand and givest freely. Thou art the bread of life, of which any may eat freely; Thou art the living water, of which we may drink without money or price.

11. Thou art the Bruiser of the Serpent's Head.

By Thee, O Christ of God, Jesus of Nazareth, who didst die, and rise again, as the sin-bearer, the great enemy of God and man is to be destroyed. Thou hast gone forth conquering, and to conquer. By Thee Satan is cast out, and cast down, and bruised under our feet[4] (Rom. 16:20). By Thee is he to be overthrown, in the last great battle between heaven and hell; and by Thee is he to be bound in chains in the abyss of fire (Rev. 20:1-10). Thou art conqueror; such a conqueror as all the potentates of evil shall not be able to confront; such a conqueror as makes our own victory sure. The conquered One, yet the conqueror; the bruised One, yet the bruiser: conquering by being conquered, bruising by being bruised. The bruising of Thy heel was the bruising of the serpent's head.

This paradox or contradiction in the first promise must have struck those who heard it, and those who heard it, and those who in after ages received it. There was a mystery that required solution, and the only key to the solution was the institution of sacrifice; the inscription on each patriarchal altar was, 'Thou shall bruise His heel, He shall bruise thy head.' The altar was the symbol of the battle; it was the battlefield itself. There the two battles were to be fought, and the two victories won: the first battle going against the woman's seed; and the second, or final one, in His favor, by the complete overthrow of the serpent, or man's great enemy. It was to be waged not between God and man, nor between Satan and man, but between God and Satan; or God personified in the Christ, and man's enemy personified in Satan, and man's enemy personified in Satan and symbolized in the serpent: man being, as it were, the prize of trophy of the fight between the Son of God and the foe of man.

On the results of the transaction done at that altar, man's eternal welfare was to turn. The Son of God went there first to be bruised, and then to bruise. It was a peculiar battle, and a peculiar victory. At that altar there were the blood, the fire, the smoke, the ashes, and the incense — all indicating the mysterious process by which the first promise was to be wrought out. Each of these had to be studied aright, in order that the sinner might understand how the bruised

One could be the bruiser, how the vanquished was to be conqueror, how death was to win life. The mystery of sin-bearing could not then be fully comprehended, but some light was shed upon it. The sinner who brought the lamb and who shed its blood at the altar, waiting to see every part of the process carried out, and the victim consumed to ashes went away satisfied with what had been done; disturbing by having given his burden to the priest, and seen it laid upon that altar; relieved in conscience and delivered in spirit by having seen the devouring fire consume the offering, leaving nothing but the *ashes*, in token that the fire had spent itself upon the victim, and that righteous wrath had righteously passed away from himself.

'There is no condemnation to them that are in Christ Jesus,' was the real meaning of every sacrifice. The bruised One has triumphed; the dying One has won the sinner's victory. 'Christ hath redeemed us from the curse of the law, being made a curse for us.' For He could only redeem the accursed one by taking the curse upon Himself. He could only save the sinner by taking the sin upon Himself.

12. Thou art the Redeemer.

In Thee we have *redemption* through Thy blood, the forgiveness of sins according to the riches of Thy grace. Thou hast *redeemed* us to God by Thy blood; and we know that our Redeemer liveth. Thou hast brought us back from the enemy; Thou hast found a ransom for us, and leadest us out of prison. Thou hast made us *redemption*

(1 Cor. 1:30); Thou hast obtained eternal *redemption* for us (Heb. 9:12). The *redemption* of the soul, the *redemption* of the body, the *redemption* of the purchased possession — all this is Thine, the work of Thy love and we are 'sealed unto the day of *redemption.*'

This *redemption* was completed on the cross; there the price was paid and the ransom found. The burial and resurrection added nothing to the redeeming work; they were but the evidence and seal of its completeness. In suffering, the just for the unjust, Christ did it all. The cross was our redemption. The cross was our justification. In that cross we have power, and life, and blessing. Christ crucified is the power of God; and to the cross we turn for strength in the day of weakness; we glory in it, for by it the world is crucified to us, and we unto the world. Redemption and power are associated together as truly as redemption and deliverance; and it is at the cross of Christ that we find these. By His stripes we are healed. By His death we live. By His blood we are redeemed; as it is written, we are 'justified freely by His grace, through the *redemption* that is in Christ Jesus' (Rom. 3:24). The apostle speaks of the day of redemption as a day still future. (Eph. 4:30). And so it is. For not until *resurrection* is redemption really completed.

Yet we may say there are two ways of redemption: the first, that which began it — on the cross, the second, that which is to finish it — at the resurrection — when He comes to raise the dead and change the living saints. To the first of these faith looks back trustingly; to the second, hope looks forward joyfully. The ransom, in virtue of which we are redeemed, was paid upon the *cross*; the redemption, which is the completion of the end for which the ransom was given, still awaits *resurrection.* For redemption in its full sense means the actual accomplishment of the thing contemplated — the full deliverance of the objects for whom the ransom was paid. Redemption from Egypt or Babylon refers to the actual recovery of the bondsmen, redemption from the bondsmen, and redemption from the power of the grave to the actual resurrection. 'I will ransom them from the power of the grave; I will redeem them from death, O death, I will be thy plaques; O grave, I will be thy destruction: repentance shall be hid from mine eyes' (Hos. 13:14).

Our connection with this redemption is, like the whole of our connection with the person or work of the Christ of God, a very simple one. It is that expressed in these words: 'He that *believeth* is not condemned' (John 3:18). 'He that heareth my word, and *believeth* on Him that sent me, hath everlasting life, and shall not come into condemnation, but is passed from death unto life' (John 5:24). 'By His *knowledge* (i.e. by the knowledge of Himself) shall my righteous Servant justify many' (Isa. 53:11). 'He that *believeth* that Jesus is the Christ is born of God' (1 John 5:1).

The Christ of God is our Redeemer, and it is by believing that we get possession of His redemption for ourselves.

Concerning this redemption, the Holy Spirit has fully spoken; and we know that His testimony is true, for it is the testimony of God that cannot lie. In receiving this divine testimony, we become connected with the redemption and the Redeemer. Not by waiting, or working, or buying, or deserving, do we get this whole redemption and the whole Redeemer, but simply by believing. 'He that *believeth*' — this is the way in which God has always put His gospel. 'He that *believeth*' is the proclamation which He commands us to make. Are we content with this? Or do we say it is too simple to be true? Surely we cannot be delivered and justified by simply believing! Well, go and dispute the matter with God, and ask Him His reasons for putting it so simply. Persuade Him to mystify His language, and alter His terms. But, until you have succeeded in pouring from Him the changes which *you* think would make it a better and safer gospel, it would be well for you to take it as it is. You are not likely to improve it; and to render it more complex in its terms would only place it beyond the reach of sinners who, sensible of total impotence and unworthiness, find it in its simplicity the only good news suitable to their case.

13. Thou art the Savior of the World.

Thou, O Jesus of Nazareth, hast come to seek and save that which was *lost*. Thy name is 'Savior, Christ the Lord' (Luke 2:11); 'God my Savior,' (Luke 1:47); the 'Savior of the world' (John 4:42); 'God our Savior' (1 Tim. 1:1). 'Our Savior Jesus Christ' (1 Tim. 1:10). Salvation is linked with Thy name, Thy person, Thy work,

Thy life, Thy death, Thy resurrection. Savior of the lost, we owe Thee, O Christ of God.

'Who hath *saved* us' is the song we sing (2 Tim 1:9); to Him who is 'able to *save* to the uttermost' (Heb. 7:25). He 'came into the world to *save* sinners' (1 Tim. 1:15). 'The Son of man came to seek and to *save* that which was lost' (Matt. 18:11); and 'by grace we are *saved,* through faith' (Eph 2:5). We preach Christ the Savior of sinners, and say: 'Believe in the Lord Jesus Christ, and thou shalt be *saved*' (Acts 16:30); for there is no salvation in any other, nor any other name given under heaven, whereby we must be saved (Acts 4:12). As the *deliverer*, He saves. As the *looser of bonds*, He saves. As the *forgiver*, He saves. As the *justifier*, He saves. As the *shepherd*, He saves. As the *quickener,* He saves. As the *propitiation*, He saves. The whole completeness of that which we call salvation is to be found in Him, without stint, or lack, or grudging. In His fullness is salvation, just such as a lost one needs — deliverance from all evil and the possession of all good.

His willingness to communicate what He possesses is as boundless as his fullness. He loves to give; nay, He giveth to all men liberally, and upbraideth not. He is clothed with the garments of *salvation* (Isa. 61:10), and He delights to impart that *salvation* to all who need it. Out of His lips goeth the word of salvation (Acts 13:26), that all who come within the sound of His voice may hear and live (Isa 55:3). He is the author of eternal *salvation* (Heb. 5:9), and He presents Himself as such to the lost. His long-suffering is *salvation* (2

Pet. 3:15); for He waits upon the sinner, not willing that any should perish, but that all should come to repentance. His Holy Scriptures are able to make us wise unto *salvation*, through faith which is in Himself (2 Tim 3:15). The Father hath 'set Him to be a light of the Gentiles, that He should be for *salvation* unto the ends of the earth' (Acts 13:47). Thus, then, He speaks to us, and says: 'Look unto me, and be ye *saved*, all the ends of the earth' (Isa. 45:22). This is the salvation and this is the Savior of whom we preach, in preaching 'the Christ of God.' Christ Jesus came into the world to *save* sinners is our message — and how shall we escape if we neglect so great *salvation*?

All that salvation is we do not, cannot know now; but we shall know hereafter. There is so much to be saved from; there is such manifold fullness in the Savior; and there is, over and above the mere salvation, such a glory, and honor, and blessedness in reserve for the saved, that we may truly say that we know not, and shall never fully comprehend, what salvation is. The 'wells of salvation' (Isa 12:3) are very deep. The heights of salvation are very lofty. The circle of salvation is very large. The joy of salvation is satisfying and exuberant. And all this is so free and rich, that we can only say it is infinitely worth the having; all things which have seen, or ear hath heard, are not to be compared with it. He who gains it gains all that is worth having; he who loses it, loses everything, and is left inconceivably and eternally poor.

14. *Thou art the Resurrection and the Life.*

The Christ of God was to be the conqueror of death and the spoiler of the grave. Through Him the old sentence of death was to be reversed, and life both for soul and body was to be restored. He came to abolish death, and bring life and immorality to light; to bind the strong man, and to spoil his house; to destroy death, and to lead captivity captive. The expression 'I am the resurrection and the life' carries us to the apostles statement as to the dead and living saints at the Lord's coming. 'He that believeth in me,' says our Lord, 'though he were dead, yet shall he live,' is similar to the words, 'The dead in Christ shall rise first.' 'He that liveth and believeth in me' (*i.e.* the living saints, or 'we who are alive and remain unto the coming of the Lord') 'shall never die,' resembles 'We shall not all sleep, but we shall all be changed,' or as it is written again, 'We that are alive and remain shall be caught up together into the clouds, to meet the Lord in the air; and so shall we be forever with the Lord' (see 1 Cor. 15. and 1 Thess. 5.)

Very great importance is attached in Scripture to *resurrection*; redemption is incomplete without it. The work of Christ fails in one main part of its reversal of Satan's work, if it does not accomplish this. Hence, He Himself reiterates the words so often, 'I will raise him up at the last day.' The theological tendencies in our day are either to deny it or to undervalue it. And hence the special value of our Lord's peculiar refutation of the Sadducees, when he quoted the words, 'I am the God of Abraham,' in proof of *resurrection,* and added, 'God is not the God of the dead, but the God of the living' (Matt. 22:32).

Some have wondered why our Lord should select such a passage as proof in this case. But first of all, it was needful in arguing with the Sadducees to look back to *Moses* for his proof; and secondly, it was needful to take words which should go down to the very root of the doctrine, and exhibit its basis as resting on the very being of God, on His relationship to His creatures, on His character as the living One, on the impossibility of His being the God of the dead. As Abraham's God, He was as much pledged to deliver Abraham's body as his soul. Resurrection was as essential a part of redemption as forgiveness and regeneration. The restoration of *every good thing* that man had lost was necessary to the fulfillment of God's eternal purpose, and was inseparably connected with the character and work of Him who came not simply as our propitiation, but our substitute, taking on Him our infirmities that He might deliver us from them, going down into our grave that He might pluck us thence; and purchasing for us bodies like His own, glorious and incorruptible.

Whether we are able just now to apprehend the full value of resurrection or not, matters little, God evidently lays great stress upon it, and seems to intimate that, without this, His great scheme would be mutilated. Many say, Oh if we be eternally blest, what matters it whether we have bodies or not? Nay, but, O man, art thou that repliest against God, undervaluing thy body which God created, and thereby affirming that this material part of creaturehood was a needless act of power, or perhaps a mistake?

It is a curious phenomenon, that in proportion as philosophic materialism makes progress in our day, resurrection is underrated or ridiculed. One would have thought that materialism would have welcomed the doctrine of resurrection as in sympathy with itself. Not so. It dislikes resurrection; especially, no doubt, because, the superhuman and supernatural are thus called in; but also because, while affirming the existence of matter, resurrection assumes the existence spirit. In other words, the material is based upon the spiritual; and resurrection implies a totally different kind of materialism from that which modern skepticism has advocated.

The connection of resurrection *with Christ* renders the reconciliation with materialism impossible. 'Jesus and the resurrection' was what the apostles preached (Acts 17:18). The two things are so linked together, that they who might be inclined to take the one without the other cannot. They must take both or none.

It is difficult to see why resurrection is so little dwelt upon by Christians. If the soul is safe, they say, we need not care what becomes of the body. God's thoughts, however, on this matter are not ours. His estimate of the body is not low and poor. When He shall transform and glorify us, then it shall be seen what the body is, to what honor it can attain, and what high functions and services to the soul it can perform. As the 'vile body' or 'body of humiliation' (Phil. 3:21), it may often seem now a hindrance, a drag, and a deformity;

but in the day when it shall be made like unto the glorious body (or body of the glory) of Him who is the resurrection and the life, it will be seen in its full serviceableness, and perfection, and beauty; the handmaid of the soul and the minister of God; the golden link or communication between the material and the spiritual, the visible and the invisible; that wondrous agency by which the will draws all precious things out of what we call nature — music from the air by touch, sweetness from substances by taste, beauty out of the stone by sculpture, power out of the fire, and fertility out of the barren soil. For the uses of the body, in its different members and senses, are beyond number, and altogether wonderful; and what we see of their uses now, is nothing in comparison with what we shall see hereafter, when God himself takes up the human frame, and as from a well-tuned harp draws out of it the melodies of the everlasting age.

We should prize resurrection. It is the true day of meeting and reunion, the day of perfection and blessedness. Then that which is sown in weakness shall be raised in power. Voices long dumb shall speak again. Eyes long dimmed shall once look into each other again. Hands shall once more clasp each other — and the long, long day of human fellowship shall begin, never to change or end. 'Awake and sing, ye that dwell in dust; for thy dew is as the dew of herbs' (Isa. 26:19).

Of this fair prospect the Christ of God is the center. 'Because I live, ye shall live also.' We rise because He has risen. We live because He liveth, His incorruption is ours; and His glory is our glory. All that we shall have in that resurrection day we shall owe to Him alone who died for us, and who rose again. Faith knits us to His cross. Faith links us to His grave. Faith connects us with His resurrection in the fullness of its eternal love and power. Through Him who is our resurrection we shall know what it is to have death swallowed up in victory, and to sing of triumph:

O death, where is the sting?
O grave, where is thy victory?
The sting of death was sin;
The strength of sin was the law.
But thanks be to God,
Who giveth us the victory,
Through our Lord Jesus Christ.

It is of the resurrection unto glory, honor, and immortality that the apostle sings so triumphantly, inviting us to join in his song. It is the song of the first resurrection, like that which Moses and Miriam sang when the Red Sea was crossed; the song of victory over death and the grave; to which song we may add this as its completion:

Blessed are they that are called
To the marriage supper of the Lamb;
Blessed and holy is he
That hath part in the first resurrection:

On such the second death shall have no power;
But they shall be priests of God and of Christ,
And shall reign with Him a thousand years.

15. *Thou art the Judge.*

'The Father judgeth no man, but hath committed all judgment to the Son; and hath given Him authority to execute judgment also, because He is the Son of man' (John 5:22, 27). It was part of God's purpose that the world should be judged by a man; and the Christ, as the 'second man,' or 'last Adam,' has come to be the world's Judge; not now, indeed, for He is not yet judging, and He has not set up His throne of judgment (John 9:39). But still He is Judge, and as such He will come again in His glory.

'Jehovah is our Judge' was part of Israel's creed. Again He is sung of in the Psalms as Judge; Judge of the earth, and the ends thereof; Judge of the nations — as in such passages as the following:

Let the nations be glad,
Yea, sing for joy:
For Thou shalt JUDGE the people righteously,
And GOVERN the nations upon the earth (Ps. 67:4).

And again, in reference to Messiah, Asaph sings:

> *God standeth in the congregation of the mighty;*
> *He JUDGETH among the gods (Ps. 82:1)*

And once more, speaking of the coming judgment and reign, David speaks:

> *He shall JUDGE the people righteously!*
> *Let the heavens rejoice*
> *And let the earth be glad;*
> *Let the Sea roar,*
> *And the fullness thereof.*
> *Let the field be joyful,*
> *And all that is therein;*
> *Then shall all the trees of the wood rejoice*
> *Before the Lord!*
> *For He cometh!*
> *For He cometh!*
> *To JUDGE the earth:*
> *He shall JUDGE the world with righteousness,*
> *And the people with His truth (Ps. 96:10-13).*

It is to JUDGMENT that all things are now pointing forward; and the coming of the Judge who is the Christ of God is the world's great hope. Like that of the ancient judges in Israel, His office is not one, but manifold. They raised up to clear the land of enemies, to sit in judgment, and to reign as kings. So shall it be with our Judge. And for Him, as such we look. The Church looks for Him; the world looks for Him; creation looks for Him. In Him, God's great original purpose concerning earth will be carried out. He comes to set up His throne, take the reins of government, and to rule in righteousness. Men shrink from such a crisis in earth's history as the arrival of the Judge implies. They dread the judgment, and they have begun to disbelieve and deny it.

That 'God will judge the world in righteousness by that Man whom He hath appointed' (Acts 17:31), is a doctrine counted obsolete by many. The current of the age is against it. The march of intellect has superseded the necessity for it. The larger and wider views of God's character now evolving show that He is not likely thus to arraign His creatures before His bar. Man, with His progress in science, and his skill in art, is getting too powerful to be thus summarily dealt with!

With many in our day, judgment by the direct interference of God is considered out of the question. Man's own indiscretions may injure him. His follies may average themselves upon him. He may thus be self-judged and self-punished, as his conscience troubles him, or as he reaps the fruit of his misdeeds. But beyond these effects of his conduct — the recoil of his own violence — judgment cannot be. It is unphilosophical, unnatural, and in the teeth of the world's history. There will be earthquakes, with submerged cities; but these are the evolution of the laws of nature. There will be the sweeping hurricane, leveling the works of man. There will be the tempest, raising the billows and swallowing up navies. There will be the lightening, splitting rocks and towers. There will be pestilence, prosecuting its remorseless march over sea and land, from east to west. There will be the famine, emptying cities and villages of their millions. There will be all these; but these are not judgment, nor forerunners of the Judge! They are the unfolding of certain rigid laws, which have been impressed on nature from the beginning, and cannot be interfered with. Beyond these agencies of terror there is no judgment, and no penalty for man's guilt!

Thus speaks philosophy, more and more boldly every year. Prosecuting the devious speculations of unbelief, it gets further and further from God. It hates the thought of God coming nearer man, either to punish or reward. 'Where is the promise of His coming?' Is its boasting shout.

Yet the Judge will come. The Christ will come. He waits, because He is long-suffering, not willing that any should perish, but that all should come to repentance. He lingers because He loves. He is slow to leave the throne of grace and to ascend the throne of judgment. For His mercy endureth forever; and every part of creaturehood is of value in His eyes. What a gospel this *delay* preaches to the sons of men, even when not a word is spoken! He lingers and tarries, because He pities, and seeks not to destroy, but to save. Each hour's delay is a fresh message of grace to you, O man! It says to you: Tarry not, draw near, be reconciled, enter into peace through the blood of the covenant, and live forever.

16. *Thou art the King of kings.*

In God's purpose there was a King. One will was to be ruler of many wills. One man was to have dominion over earth and sea. In heaven there seems to be no such predominance or preeminence of the one over the many. God there is all, and under Him directly the heavenly hosts. On earth it was otherwise. God was to rule it by means of a man, and the first Adam was set on its throne as sole and sovereign ruler. Earth was given to man to be *ruled* by him, as well as to be replenished.

The first man left his estate and lost his crown. Since then there have been many rulers among the many subdivisions of regions of earth. And these rulers man has called kings. For many ages they have been exercising dominion, yet they have failed to rule successfully. Earth is no nearer its normal state of order and peace than it was when first they took up their scepters. Nay, under the ruler of man, confusion multiples; lawlessness and disobedience overflow; and nothing but the sword prevents this world from being a chaos and a slaughter house. The armies of earth, meant for war, are the only preservers of peace.

God means to prove to the uttermost, and to test his ability to govern and to preserve order on his own earth. When that proof has been completed, and man demonstrated to be unable to rule his own world, then God introduces His own King, who is to rule the earth in righteousness.

This King of kings is the Christ of God. Times without number has God described for us this Messiah and his kingdom — His fitness to reign, and the glory, as well as the peace and order, by which that reign is to be distinguished.

Thus David speaks in his last words:

> *There shall be a just one ruling over men,*
> *Ruling in the fear of God.*
> *He shall be as the light of the morning.*
> *When the sun riseth;*
> *A morning without clouds (Sam. 23:4).*

Thus he speaks in the well-known psalm of the kingdom:

> *Give the King Thy judgments, O God,*
> *And Thy righteousness unto the King's Son.*
> *He shall judge Thy people with righteousness,*
> *And Thy poor with judgment.*
> *In His days shall the righteous flourish;*
> *And abundance of peace shall be*

As long as the moon endureth.
He shall have dominion from sea to sea,
And from the river to the ends of the earth.
All kings shall fall down before Him;
And all nations shall serve Him (Ps. 72 1-11).

Thus, too, Isaiah points the prophetic finger to the coming King — the expected Christ:

Behold!
A King shall reign in righteousness,
And princes shall decree judgment.
Yea, this man shall be
A hiding-place from the wind,
And a covert from the tempest;
As rivers of water in a dry place,
As the shadow of a great rock in a weary land
(Isa. 32:1)

And again he points to Him, and dilates upon the glories of His reign of peace, the 'restitution of all things,' the more than restoration of Paradise:

There shall come forth a rod.
Out of the stem of Jesse,

And a branch (a shoot)

Shall grow out of his roots:

And the spirit of the Lord shall rest upon Him,

The spirit of wisdom and understanding,

The spirit of counsel and might,

The spirit of knowledge and of the fear of the Lord.

With righteousness shall He judge the poor,

And reprove with equity for the meek of the earth:

And He shall smite the earth

With the rod of His mouth,

And with the breath of His lips

Shall He slay the wicked.

And righteousness shall be the girdle of His loins,

And faithfulness the girdle of His reins.

The wolf also shall dwell with the lamb,

And the leopard shall lie down with the kid;

The calf, the young lion, and the fatling together;

And a little child shall lead them.

And the cow and the bear shall feed;

Their young ones shall lie down together:

And the lion shall eat straw like the ox.

The suckling child shall play on the hole of the asp,

And the weaned child shall put his hand on the cock-atrice' den.

They shall not hurt nor destroy

In all my holy mountain:
For the earth shall be full
Of knowledge of the Lord,
As the waters cover the sea (Isa 11:1-9).

His crown, His throne, His sceptre, are fully described in many ways, and by different prophets; each seeming to vie with the other as to who shall speak of them most perfectly. Messiah as King is one of the most prominent themes of prophecy. We find Him everywhere as such — the Church's joy, the world's hope, Israel's expectation, and creation's deliverance. And when He comes again in His royal splendor, we read:

In righteousness doth He judge and make war.
His eyes were as a flame of fire,
And on His head are many crowns;
And he is clothed with a vesture dipped in blood:
And His name is called THE WORD OF GOD.
Out of His mouth goeth a sharp sword,
That with it He should smite the nations;
And He shall rule them with a rod of iron:
And He threadeth the wine press
Of the fierceness and wrath
Of Almighty God.
And He hath on His vesture and on His thigh

A name written,

Kings of kings and Lord of lords (Rev. 19:11-15).

Messiah is at once Priest and King. His is the royal priesthood, or the priestly kingship. He is Melchizedek, King of Salem, and Priest of the Most High God. His kingdom is an everlasting kingdom. As son of Adam, His dominion is over earth; as son of David, His kingdom is over Israel. Yet is He King of heaven also, seated on the eternal throne, and wearing the crown of the universe. For there is a future for the Church, a future for Israel, a future for the earth, a future for heaven, a future for the universe in connection with His kingship as the Christ of God, which is as blessed as it is boundless, as glorious as it is eternal.

On His throne shall His Church sit, sharing His triumphs and glories; for each of His redeemed is an heir of God, and a joint-heir with Christ. 'If we suffer, we shall also reign with Him.' Our designation is 'partakers of the glory that shall be revealed.' The lines have fallen unto us in pleasant places; yea, we have a goodly heritage. We eat of the tree of life, which is in the midst of the paradise of God. We receive the crown of righteousness (Tim. 4:8), the crown of life (Jas. 1:12), the crown of Glory (1 Pet. 5:4). Ours is the morning star; and having overcome, we sit with Messiah on His throne, even as He overcame and sat down with the Father on His throne.

CHAPTER 6

WHAT FOLLOWS THIS OBESSION

This obsession cannot be barren. It contains in it such truth as must be productive in many ways. All truth is indeed fruitful according to its kind, but this is the most fruitful of all.

It contains, besides, so much personal truth — truth which we need, and truth which could not be reached in any other way. Its effect upon us is marvelous. Its teachings are as manifold as they are divine. It wraps up within it so many other truths, that in getting hold of it we find ourselves in possession of 'unsearchable riches.'

1. *I see in Thee the Love of God.*

It is especially with this we have to do; for without this, man must be poor and dark — a land without a stream — a world without a sun. Messiah is (1) the gift of God's love, (2) the embodiment of God's love, (3) the pledge of God's love, (4) the measure of God's love. I read in Thy person, Thy words, Thy doings, Thy life, Thy death, that 'God is love.' It is of the love of Godhead that Thou hast brought us the glad tidings; for the Father sent Thee to announce His love. 'God so loved the world, that He gave His only begotten Son.' Love shineth in Thee; not merely love such as heaven needs, but such as earth needs — love such as is needed by the unlovable and the unworthy — the love of forgiveness, and reconciliation, and peace — the love of God which is in Christ Jesus our Lord. Thy birth spoke of love. Thy life spoke of love. Thy words spoke of love. Thy miracles spoke of love. All Thy footsteps spoke of love. And Thy death was the death of love. It was the love of God that shone down from Thy cross upon earth, like a new-lighted sun. The love of the cradle was much; the love of the cross was more. In Thee, the Christ of God, we learn the love of God.

2. *I see in Thee my Way of Access to God.*

Through Thee, O Christ, I have access by one Spirit unto the Father. Thou hast drawn nigh to me, that I might draw nigh to Thee and to the Father. Thou hast prepared a way; nay, Thou art Thyself the new and living Way. Thou art the altar and the layer by which I pass into the holy place. Thou art the incense, the perfume of which makes me acceptable in the courts of the Lord. Thou art the veil which was rent in twain, that I might enter into the holiest. Thou art the mercy seat, the throne of grace to which I am to come boldly, with a true heart, and in the full assurance of faith. Through Thee I have access with boldness, and everything in Thee assures me that all that might have repelled or discouraged me has been removed. The greatness of my sins cannot shut me out, for Thy blood cleanseth from all sin. The distance to which I have gone from God need be no discouragement, for by Thee we are brought nigh. Thou art the Way the Truth, and the Life. Through Thee, I, though exceeding sinful, go to God, worship in His holy place, and have communion with Himself. I heard the voice from the rent veil, which says, 'Let us draw near,' and I draw near. It is now not danger, but safety, to go in. My guilt is not in entering, but in refusing to enter; not in being bold, but in refusing to be bold, and my presumption is not in believing, but in doubting; not in simply crediting the word of God, and the record which He has given of His Son, but in setting aside that record, and making Him a liar.

3. *I see in Thee the Forgiveness of Sins.*

Forgiveness! That was, if not the words, at least the meaning, of the first promise concerning Thee, the seed of the woman. 'Forgiving iniquity, transgression, and sin,' was Thy name of old to Israel, and it is so still to us. Thy hast come to earth as the Christ, with forgiveness in Thy hand; forgiveness from the Father; forgiveness, free as the sunshine which Thou daily makest to arise upon us; forgiveness, without a grudge, or price, or reservation. I hear the cry from the cross, 'Father, forgive them;' and from that I learn Thine errand to us. I mark Thy words to the guilty woman, 'Neither do I condemn thee,' and from them I understand Thy pardoning grace. Thou cleanest from all unrighteousness, and turnest the scarlet into snow, the crimson into wool. Through Thee is preached unto us the forgiveness of sins! Through Thee there is no condemnation for us, so that we can take up the apostle's challenge joyfully, and say, 'Who is he that comdemneth?'

4. I see in Thee my Justification.

In Thee I am more than pardoned; I am justified freely by Thy blood. I am partaker of a divine righteousness, so that all my imperfection vanishes, and becomes invisible in the glory of Thy perfection. In Thee, the Christ of God, I find not merely the Just One taking the place of the unjust, that the penalty might be remitted, and the wrath removed; but I find the Just so substituting Himself for the unjust, that the unjust rises to the judicial level of the Just, and is dealt with by God as if he were the just One, possessing the excellence of His righteousness, and standing before God in His divine beauty. This is the fullness of that justification which we receive from Thee when we believe in Thee, consenting to take Thee as our substitute, and to be received by God according to the merits of Thee, the Christ, the son of the living God. O Christ, I take Thee as my righteousness, my justification, my perfection, and gladly give up every claim of my own, hiding myself beneath Thy robe, and being 'found in Thee,' 'complete in Thee,' 'accepted in the Beloved.'

5. *I see in Thee my Life Eternal.*

I take Thee as my life, for I am all death; and the life which I find in Thee is everlasting *life*. Because Thou livest, I live, and shall live. *Life* eternal! That is what I need; and of Thee, O Christ, I find it written, 'This is the true God, and eternal *life*' (1 John 5:20); nay, I find it also written, 'This is the record, that God hath given to us eternal *life*; and this *life* is in His Son. He that hath the Son hath *life*; he that hath not the Son of God hath not *life*' (1 John 5:11, 13). Again and again didst Thou speak of the *life* that is in Thee, and of that *life* as presented to us, that we might have it — have it in receiving the Father's testimony to Thee. We have heard Thy voice, telling us of this life, and all its blessedness; putting to our lips the vessel containing it, that we might have both Thy love and the nearness of the proffered gift. We take the gift, so earnestly and so sincerely pressed upon us; and as those whose portion was death we accept the blessed exchange, and enter into life through Thee, the living One, the Son of the living God. Thou art the tree of life; and under Thy shadow I sit down to eat Thy pleasant fruit. Thou art the bread of life; and on Thee would I daily feed, as Israel on their morning manna. Thou art the water of life; and of Thee would I drink every hour and moment, that I may thirst no more, and thirst forever!

6. *I see in Thee my Peace.*

Thou art the Peacemaker. Yes, Thou art the *Peace*: as it is written, He hath made *peace* by the blood of His cross; He is our *peace*; and Thy name is the 'Son of *peace*' (Luke 10:6), the 'Lord of peace' (2 Tim 3:16), the 'Prince of *peace*' (Isa. 9:6). There was distance between God and me; there was variance, nay, enmity; but Thou hast removed these, and the quarrel is at an end forever. Thy blood speaketh peace to me, and it keeps my soul in peace. When sin comes in, and threatens to break it up, I betake myself to Thee. I go back to the place where I found it at first, and I find it there again. The cross stands immovable. The value of the blood never changes: it is always able to do the same thing for us to the end that it did at first; and to those who accept God's testimony to that blood, all its value belongs, unfailing and unchangeable. The value of that blood is my security for abiding peace. Were its value less than divine, my peace would be both imperfect and insecure. Today it might be peace, tomorrow disquietude and doubt; today nearness, tomorrow distance. But the value of the blood is infinite, and avails forever for all who stand not aloof from it, or undervalue its efficacy. Our peace offering has been offered once for all, and its efficacy is everlasting. We have not to present a new peace offering for ourselves of any kind whatever — the peace offering of our prayers, or tears, or repentances, or almsdeeds, or fervent feelings, or attractive rites. Thou, O Christ, art our one peace offering; and we take Thee as such, not trying to make again a peace already made, but satisfied with Thee as all we need for the maintaining of that peace which can only rest upon reconciling blood.

7. *I see in Thee my Health.*

'Thou hast *healed* me,' were the words of an Old Testament saint; and again we have other words like them, 'He *healeth* all thy diseases' (Ps. 103:3). The first Adam was the destroyer of our *health*, the last Adam is the restorer of it. As healer both of body and soul, Thou did not show Thyself when here, O Christ of God, ever healing, ever soothing, ever comforting — ever administering Thy balm of Gilead! True healer of the soul! True strengthener of the weak! True physician of the sick! True light of the sickroom, and compassion of the sickbed! Thy fellowship is healing. Thy words are healing. Thy touch is healing. Thy love is healing. Long ere Thou camest to earth, Thy people knew of Thy *healing* skill and power. Often didst Thou *heal* Thy Israel, in Thy great love and pity; and when healing the bitter waters of Marah, Thou didst proclaim Thyself the *healer* of Israel: 'I am Jehovah that healeth thee' (Ex. 15:26). O health of the soul, show Thyself to me in all Thy fullness; heal me more and more. Heal my understanding, heal my conscience, and heal my heart. Let that be true of me which was written concerning Thy healing wonders of old, 'As many as touched Him were made perfectly whole.' I am as yet but very imperfectly recovered; slowly,

slowly am I returning to spiritual health. Oh, hasten the desired end, intensify Thy medicines, put more vigour into Thy touch, make my recovery more rapid, perfect that which concerneth me; oh, heal me, and I shall be healed!

8. I see in Thee my Wisdom.

Thou, O Christ of God, art the *wisdom* of God; and I am wise in Thee. Thy hidden treasures are all open to me, and I am welcome to search every chamber of Thy storehouse, and to appropriate all that is there. 'The world by wisdom knew not God (1 Cor. 1:21); but by Thy wisdom I am made acquainted with God. I say, Show me the Father, and Thou showest Him to me. I lack wisdom, and I ask of Thee; and Thou givest liberally, and upbraidest not. All *wisdom* is in Thee, and I may have it all. Thou teachest, and Thou art also the lesson taught. I have come into Thy school, for the door was open; I have sat down there upon its benches as a scholar, and Thou didst not frown upon me. Oh, then, teach me, teach me! I am weary of other teachers. They profit nothing. They cannot reach the recesses of my dull and unteachable heart. They are impatient, and will take no pains with my ignorance and stupidity. But Thou art different. Thou teachest the inner man, Thou art always pitying and loving, never impatient because of my ignorance, nor fretted at my forwardness. Thou takest such pains with me, day by day, as if I were Thy only scholar. O teach me more and more!

9. I see in Thee my Captain.

Thou leadest me on to victory; for Thy name is Captain of Jehovah's hosts. I will follow whither Thou leadest. 'Be of good cheer, I have overcome the world,' is the watchword which Thou givest us. And thou goest before us to the battlefield, and marshalls all our array. Thou givest us the whole armour of God — the sword of the Spirit, the helmet of salvation, the girdle of truth, the breast-plate of righteousness, the shield of faith; for every soldier in Thy host is well-armed and disciplined, able to withstand in the evil day, and having done all, to stand. My foes are many and fierce; I have no strength against them; no skill with which to cope with their skill and stratagem. Captain of Jehovah's host, lead me on to victory. The promises are to him that overcometh; oh, help me to fight and overcome, that I may win the prize. Enable me to war the good warfare, to fight the good fight. There are fightings without, and fears within; but lead me on. The principalities and powers of hell come against me, the rulers of the darkness of this world; but Thou art mightier than they; make them to flee before me. I would choose no other commander; I put myself at Thy disposal; order the array for me, and make me more than conqueror through Him that loved me.

10. I see in Thee Him whom I must love.

The Christ of God is the infinitely lovable one, the chief among ten thousand. All beauty, all perfection, all excellence, are on Thee, O Christ. There is none like Thee among the sons of men; neither is there any love like Thy love. Thou art He whom the Father loveth, and He whom the Father loveth must be worthy of my love. Thou lovest us, and shall we not love Thee? Thou gavest Thy life for us, and shall we not love Thee? Thou didst rise from the dead for us, and shall we not love Thee? Altogether lovely art Thou; and we give Thee love, as the only one worthy of it. There is nothing in Thee but what is attractive; all that Thou hast said and done is fitted to command our love. Help me to love Thee; to love Thee perfectly; to love Thee more and more; to requite Thy love with mine; and to show my love to Thee by the devotedness of my daily life. If I love Thee not, all is wrong with me. Oh, set me right, and shed abroad Thy love in my heart, that I may render Thee my best and warmest affections. Thou askest me the threefold question once asked of a denying disciple, 'Lovest thou me?' Oh, teach me to answer with the same confidence as he did, even in the full remembrance of his sad denial: 'Yea, Lord, Thou knowest all things, Thou knowest that I love Thee.'

11. I see in Thee One whom I can trust.

What I have heard and known of Thee, O Christ of God, makes me feel that Thou art infinitely *trustworthy.* I can *trust* Thine arm, for it is strong. I can trust Thy guidance, for it is sure. I can trust Thy guardianship, for it is almighty. I can trust Thy light, for it is the light of heaven. I can trust Thy rod and staff, for they lead and guide aright. I can trust Thy shade in the day of heat, for it is the shadow of a great rock in a weary land. I can trust Thy patience, for it is perfect. I can trust Thy words, for they are true and faithful. I can trust Thy love, for it passeth knowledge. Oh, help me to trust Thee more! Why should a suspicion ever cross me? Why should any distrust ever find its way into my soul? Why should I not know at all times what is confidence in Thee, the Son of the living God, the lover of the lost, helper of the helpless, the healer of the sick, the succourer of the poor, the uplifter of the fallen, the rest of the weary? Let Thy perfect love cast out fear, for fear hath torment; and he that feareth does not comprehend this perfect love of Thine. Let me hear the gracious words ever sounding in my ears: Trust ye in the Lord forever, for in the Lord Jehovah is everlasting strength. I will trust and not be afraid.

12. *I see in Thee One whom I must worship.*

Thy name is Jehovah, and Thou art God over all, blessed forever. Thou wert 'in the beginning,' Thou wert with God, and Thou wert God. All things were made by Thee, and without Thee was not anything made that was made. Thou art the same yesterday, today, and forever. Shall I not worship and bow down before Thee? Shall I not praise Thee — not as one man praises another, but as they praise Jehovah, who worship in His temple, crying, Holy, holy, holy Lord God Almighty, the whole earth is full of Thy glory! Thy name is above every name in heaven and earth, and the glory of the universe is Thine. O Lord, our Lord, how excellent is Thy name in all the earth! Not less than God art Thou; therefore, I praise Thee. Immanuel, the Word made flesh, Son of God, and Son of man, I worship Thee. Light of the world, Light of life, Prince of kings of the earth, King of nations, King of kings and Lord of lords, I worship Thee! The heaven of heavens cannot contain Thy glory, and all creation sends up to Thee its everlasting song. I join my voice with them in adoration and extol Thee both as Creator and Redeemer; for in Thee I see Him who made all things by the word of His power, and Him who redeemed us to God by His blood. I sing, 'Worthy is the lamb that was slain to receive power, and riches, and wisdom, and strength, and honor, and glory, and blessing…Blessing, and honor, and glory, and power to Him that sitteth upon the throne and unto the Lamb forever and ever.'

13. *I see in Thee Him to whom I must consecrate myself.*

Thou art worthy of myself, and of my all. There is none like Thee in heaven or in earth. Even hadst Thou not loved me, nor done ought for me, Thy excellency is enough to lead to the consecration of myself, and of everything which I possess, to Thee. But Thou hast loved me, and therefore I give myself to Thee. Thou hast loved me with an immeasurable love, and therefore Thou must have my complete self — spirit, soul, and body. Thou hast given Thyself to me, and I give myself to Thee. Thou hast been born for me, Thou hast lived for me, Thou has died for me; and I devote my whole self perfectly to Thee, that I may serve Thee, obey Thee, follow Thee, delight in Thee. I would keep back nothing from Him who bought me with such a price, and washed me in blood so precious. I give strength to Thee; my powers and faculties; my time and health; my gold and silver; my life and my death — all I have and own I give to Thee, O Christ, Son of God, and Lord of heaven and earth. Uproot selfishness, and self-seeking, and self-glorying. God forbid that I should glory, save in Thy cross, and that I should make the object of my life anything save what in some way or measure bears upon Thy honor and subserves Thy cause. Draw me, and I will run after Thee. Make me wholly Thine, in every part of my being. Life is not life, if Thou art not its beginning and its end; nor is there any joy of earth which I ought to separate from Thee. It is not, what will man say of me? That I must ask myself, but what will Christ say? — not, how will this bear upon my own wealth, or influence, or honor? but, how will it bear upon the cause, the work, the glory of Him whose I am, and whom I serve? Be Thou ALL, in everything, small and great, private or public. Fill up my days and nights with Thyself, that no part of my time may be without Thee. In the closet, in the family, in the street, in the place of business, in solitude, in company, be Thou ever with me, and in me. In my joys and in my sorrows, in my gains and losses, in my health and in my sickness, in my silence and in my speech, in my journeying or in my resting, in my plans and in my perplexities, my conflicts, my frets and troubles, my disappointments and vexations, my waiting and weariness, my riches and poverty — in all these, be Thou with me, and I with Thee; so consecrated to Thee, that I shall feel every fragment of my life and every change of my lot a new opportunity for developing that consecration which I owe Thee, and which will give to me, not bondage and irksomeness but liberty and gladness. O Christ, help me more and more to take up my cross, to deny myself, and to follow Thee; to present my body a living sacrifice, holy, acceptable unto God unto Thee, walking in Thy steps and shining in Thy light, and bearing every burden which Thy love may lay upon me.

Set me as a seal upon Thine heart,
As a seal upon Thine arm;
For love is stronger than death,
Jealousy is cruel as the grave:

The coals thereof are coals of fire,
A most vehement flame.
Let Him kiss me with the kisses of Thy mouth,
For Thy love is better than wine.

14. I see in Thee Him for whom I must watch.

Thou art absent, and I will remember Thee; I will think upon Thee, even as Thou rememberest me, and thinkest upon me. For absence makes no difference in love. It but whets the appetite. I cannot forget what Thou wert, when here in Thy lowliness and sorrow. I cannot cease to meditate on what Thou art now in Thy exaltation. Teach me the meaning of these words: 'Whom having not seen we love; and in whom, though now we see Him not, yet believing, we rejoice with joy unspeakable and full of glory.' But this is not all. We are not content with absence. We wish to see Thy face, to hear Thy voice, and to have fellowship such as Thy disciples had when Thou wert with them — such as Moses and Elias upon the mount of transfiguration. And Thou hast promised that it shall be so. Thou wilt not be always absent. Thou hast promised to come again for us, and be with us forever. Thou hast not revealed the day or hour, so that we know not when we may expect Thee. But we love Thee and we will watch. We long to see Thee, and we will watch. We are weary of absence, and we will watch. The world is getting darker and sadder, and we will watch. Thou hast bidden us, and we will watch. It is long, long since Thou didst warn us to trim our lamps, and we will watch. The night may be nearer its end than many think, and we will watch. The world has forgotten Thee, and is occupied with its commerce and science, saying, These are thy gods, O men; therefore we will watch. The first resurrection may be nearer than we think, and we will watch. We hear Thy voice, 'He which testifieth these things saith, Surely I come quickly;' and we reply, Amen. Even so come, Lord Jesus.

CHAPTER 7

GOD'S MIGHTY WORK IN AND THROUGH THE CHURCH

'That God may be all in all' is the basis of all apostolic doctrine, from which it sets out, and into which it returns, and round and round which it revolves. 'Of Him, and through Him, and to Him, are all things,' is the refrain of the apostle's songs; a refrain which the whole early Church took up and sung with so loud a harmony, that the sound went over earth, and pagan nations awoke, startled at the name of the living and true God, King eternal, immortal, and invisible, the only wise God, so different from their Jupiter, their Mercury, and other such false and unclean gods. The burden of these doxologies is: Glory to that eternal Jehovah who worketh all in all, who filleth all in all.

God is the *doer* as we are the *purposer* of everything connected with the Christ, and of everything relating to the redeemed and their connection with the Christ, who is the center of all His purposes and desires. The Church is His creation. Each saint is His creation. There is no religion in a man save that which originates with Him, and is consummated by Him. Religion that is self-made, consisting of doctrines, feelings, rites, self-taught and self-wrought, is no better than ancient paganism. 'We are His workmanship, created in Christ Jesus unto good works, which God hath before ordained that we should walk in them' (Eph. 2:10): that is, we are His workmanship, not our own (ver.8); nay, we are His 'creation,'[1] nay, His creation *in* and *by* Christ Jesus; and all this for 'good works,' for which God had made all this vast preparation, 'that we should walk in them.'

Thus God is in Christ *purposing* concerning us; for Christ and the redeemed are inseparable in the eternal purpose of the Father. That purpose embraces both, and embodies the mutual relationship of the one to the other. It contemplates also, and makes preparation for, the holiness of each redeemed one, as well as for the perfection of the whole Church of God; as it is written, 'Who hath saved us, and called us with an holy calling, not according to our works, but according to His own purpose and grace, which was given us in Christ Jesus before the world began, but is now made manifest by the appearing of our Savior Jesus Christ' (2 Tim 1:9,10).

Thus God is in Christ *working* concerning us; for all His operations for us and in us are in connection with Christ. From the first touch of His hand, when He arrests us in our folly, to the last, when He finishes the glorious work in the resurrection of our bodies, all His doings concerning us are 'in Christ.' 'He created all things by Jesus Christ,' is as true of the new creation as of the old. He is the former of all things, the Lord of Hosts is His name. Each hour bears witness to the unceasing and unwearied touches of His hand in moulding us anew after His own image. And all this is the working and purposing of 'love' — the love of God which is in Jesus Christ our Lord. And all this to the praise of the glory of His grace, that God may be all in all.

Thus God is in Christ *reconciling* us to Himself; for the reconciliation comes through this living channel, and this only. God approaches us in Christ, lays hold on us in Christ, looks at us in Christ, makes proposals to us in Christ, and links us to Himself in Christ. 'You hath He reconciled in the body of His flesh through death' (Col. 1:22). The reconciliation of the covenant is Christ Jesus our Lord. Save in Him, there is no nearness, no favor, no friendship, and no fellowship. The one Mediator is the one reconciler, through whom God says to us, 'Come unto me;' and as there is but one mediation, one reconciliation, one cross, one blood, one death one burial, one resurrection. For in each of these Christ is all. 'He of God has made unto us wisdom, and righteousness, and sanctification, and redemption.'

Thus God is in Christ, *not imputing* unto us our trespasses; for the forgiveness of all sin comes through Him, 'in whom we have redemption through His blood, even the forgiveness of sins, according to the riches of His grace' (Col.1:14). The *non-imputation* of sin takes for granted its *existence*. It exists, but it is not imputed to us, because it has been righteously imputed to another; and that vicarious imputation has been accepted by the Judge, and is presented to us, that we, accepting it, may have all the fullness of the non-imputation or no condemnation made over to us. We acknowledge the sin to the sin bearer, that it might not be reckoned to us.

Thus God is *quickening* us; for it is written, 'God, who is rich in mercy, for the great love wherewith He loved us, even when we were dead in sins, hath *quickened us together with Christ'* (Eph. 2:4); and as He quickeneth us now with Him, so hereafter He will raise us up with Him, in the day of which He speaks, 'My dead body shall they arise' (Isa. 26:19). The life of Christ becomes our life, flows into us, flows through us, imparting to both soul and body the spiritual energy, or 'everlasting life,' contained in Him as the one fountainhead, communication both the present and eternal vitality, which, beginning in the new birth here, it to be consummated in the glories of the first resurrection, at His second coming. For it is one life, and one life giver, and one fountain of life, from first to last.

Thus God is *enlightening* us; for it is by our connection with Him who is the Light of the world that we are enlightened. 'In Him was life, and the life was the light of men' (John 1:4); and it is the light proceeding from Him which reveals God to us, and makes light to us in the Lord. That which alone is light to us is 'the light of the knowledge of the glory of God in the face of Jesus Christ.' As of the New Jerusalem hereafter, so of the Church now, and so of each believing soul, 'the Lamb is the light thereof; and the light of the Lamb is the light of the cross. The cross is our lamp. All is darkness to which the illumination of the cross does not extend. Light for the human spirit! Light for the gloom of earth! Light for the church of God! All these are to be found in the cross of Him whom God hath set forth as a 'propitiation, through faith in His blood:' for without the propitiation, of the blood light cannot come to the sinner. Heaven may not need that light, but earth does. It is through the blood of the everlasting covenant that the light streams into the soul; and it is thus that it is to stream into the New Jerusalem (Rev 21:23), filling it with redemption light forever. 'I am the Light of the world,' is the bright message that is going through earth just now, in the day of her darkness; and it is this that is to be perpetuated forever in the peculiar glory of the celestial city — a city which, through coming down from God out of heaven, is yet to have for its citizens, not angels, but men who have been redeemed with the precious blood of Christ.

Thus God is *strengthening* us. Our helplessness and the divine power meet together, and find how entirely suitable they are, each to the other. We need divine strength; for the weakness introduced into the human soul by sin is great. The divine strength needs weakness such as ours on which to show itself; for in no one case can it find occasion for coming forth in all its fullness. God's purpose — both to manifest Himself and to deliver us — -was to make us absolutely dependent on His power in every region of our being, and in every part of that mysterious process of our restoration to His image. Therefore, He strengthens us with might by His Spirit in the inner man. He makes us 'strong in the Lord, and in the power of His might;' teaching us to 'glory in our infirmities, that the peace of Christ may rest upon us.' There is strength enough in Him for us. Every day we need its fullness; every hour we are welcome to it in all its magnitude.

Thus God is *comforting* us. In the everlasting covenant, the Church is recognized as passing through much tribulation; as being in deep waters and in burning fires:

The path of sorrow, and that path alone,
Leads to the land where sorrow is unknown;
No traveler ever reached that blest abode,
Who found not thorns and briars in his road.
For He who knew what human hearts would prove,
How slow to learn the dictates of His love;
That, hard by nature, and of stubborn will,
A life of ease would make them harder still;
In pity to the souls His grace designed
To rescue from the ruins of mankind,
Called for a cloud to darken all their years
And said, Go spend them in the vale of tears.

Such was the purpose of God both concerning the discipline and the deliverance, the road through which His saints were to pass to the kingdom, and the consolation as well as companionship which they were to have upon that way. The Christ was made 'perfect through sufferings;' and so is the Church. Therefore is consolation needed; otherwise the way would be too sad, and the discipline too heavy. And a Comforter is also needed; that Comforter, the promise of the Father, sent down by Christ to sustain us in the day of His absence. He who purposed all things from the beginning, and now worketh all things according to that purpose, suits the discipline. He comforteth us in all our tribulation; nay, He makes us to glory in tribulation: for this is the road by which all the former saints went to the kingdom; the way by which all are going now; the way by which the Master went during His sojourn here.

Thus God is *purifying* us. The furnace was provided in the eternal purpose. We were not in a moment to be transferred to the glory above, as soon as we were begotten again to the lively hope. We were not to be instantaneously perfected and purified, so that sin should be utterly expelled from us, and we should have no more need of the blood, no more need of the daily discipline. God's purpose was that our preparation should be by a *process*, not by an act: that by gradual process we should be the occasion for drawing out the power and grace of God. Instantaneous perfection seems to some more glorifying to God than gradual improvement. But God does not think so. He wants to show us what sin is, what the power of evil is, what human heart is, what the blood of Christ can do, what the power of the Spirit can do. And so He purifies us gradually. He has done so from the beginning; and there is not an instance in Scripture of instantaneous perfection, nay, not one instance of perfection at all. The law of the kingdom is expressed in the following prayer of the apostle: 'The God of all grace, who hath called us unto His eternal glory by Christ Jesus, AFTER THAT YE HAVE SUFFERED A WHILE, MAKE YOU PERFECT, stablish, strengthen, settle you' (1 Pet.l 10:10).

Thus God is *making us His witnesses.* Ye are my witness, He says to us. Witness of whom? Of the Christ of God. We testify of Him; we reflect His light, we radiate His glory. We are His mirrors here. We are like the moon, giving back some of the light He sheds on us; like the sea, shinning with His brightness; like the mountains, telling of His greatness; like the wind, speaking of His power; like the flowers, displaying His beauty; like the blue arch, proclaiming His vastness; like the sands, symbolizing the years of His eternity; like the rainbow unfolding His varied perfections; like the rivers, reminding men of the ceaseless roll of His providence; like the rain, showing His refreshing bounty; like the harvest filed, displaying the exuberant fullness of His love.

Thus are we in these ways, and in a thousand more, His witness; telling out all His glory, and power, and holiness, and love. Our life is to be one continuous witness-bearing to the God and Father of our Lord Jesus Christ, and to the Christ Himself, who, when He left this earth, left us behind Him to represent Him here. Let our testimony be full; let our representation be worthy of Him whose representatives we are.

We are left here to bear witness to the Christ of God. Let us see that we do it well.

The world needs our testimony, for it knows Him not, neither cares to know Him. Let our lives be such a testimony as shall win the very worst, and attract the most distant and heedless. Let that testimony be full; let it be consistent: for who can tell the injury that has been done by inconsistent testimony — by the lives of Christians who were far more like the world that they professed to have forsaken, than the Lord to whom they had joined themselves?

The Church, too, needs consistent witness-bearing. It needs to be lifted up; and who is to lift it up? It needs to be more completely unworldly and unearthly; and who shall help to make it such? It needs to be roused and quickened; but who shall rouse and quicken it, if all be slumbering and sleeping? It needs to start upon a new career of devotedness, and fervent self-denial, and holiness, and love; but who is to begin?

CHAPTER 8

LIFE THROUGH FAITH IN THE CHRIST OF GOD

At the close of his gospel, John warns us against supposing that he had given a *complete* narrative of the words and works of the Lord Jesus (John 21:25); or that even a complete narrative could possibly be given. The grace, the glory, the number of these, were far beyond the pen or the lips of man. The speaker and the doer of these was the Infinite One; and His words and works, both in number and excellence, were like Himself.

In the conclusion of his twentieth chapter we have a statement of a similar kind to the above, and one which bears very closely upon the truths we have been endeavoring to bring out in the preceding pages concerning the Christ of God. The apostle seems afraid of allowing the very thought to enter any reader's mind for a moment, that his Gospel was to be received as a complete record of the life of the Son of God on earth. It was not such. It could not be such. It was not intended to be such. What! A short treatise of twenty-one brief chapters contains the full history of the Christ of God! Impossible! Could the hollow of a babe's hand contain the ocean?

It is with the remembrance of these things that we are to read this marvelous Gospel. It is but one star, or fragment of a star, taken out of myriads — myriads now hidden, but of all which shall one day see.

But let us take up the passage under the following points: (1) the signs; (2) the faith; (3) the life; (4) the name.

1. The Signs. — The word sign does not confine itself to miracles; nor does it refer to something future, as if it contained something prophetical. It is something which signifies that the person speaking is really the person whom he professes to be, something which identifies the individual and which verifies his statements. The turning of Moses' rod into a serpent was to be a 'sign' to Pharaoh that God had spoken to Moses. The going back of the shadow upon the dial of Ahaz was to be a sign to Hezekiah that God would heal him. The Jews asked a sign from Jesus, to prove to them that He was the Messiah.

A sign, then, in the case of Christ, was something which signified that He was really that which He professed to be. Of these signs His miracles formed the chief part, though not the whole. His resurrection from the dead was the one great sign given especially by God to prove that He was the Christ.

The proofs of the ability of that resurrection, and of the disciples of Him who was now appearing to the disciples as their *risen* Master, with Him who went out and in among them so long, and who was at last nailed to the cross, were the wounds in His hands, and feet, and side, which He now exhibited to Thomas and the rest of the of the disciples.

Of such 'signs' John had recorded many; but he intimates to us that there were many more behind, many more which he might have recorded, many more which his own memory could recall — all of them bearing upon the point of the Messiahship of Jesus; all of them *public* 'signs' too, not done in a corner, but openly, before men: 'Many other signs truly did Jesus, in the presence of His disciples, which are not written in this book.' The events in the life of Jesus may well be compared to the stars in the night skies. The eye sees many, and what we see is enough to attest the power and glory of Jehovah; the telescope shows many more; if our telescopes were enlarged and improved, we might see more still; were our powers of vision increased, or were we translated to some other sphere, we should see more and more of them, all proclaiming the might and majesty of their Maker. So with the facts in the life of Jesus. The evangelists have gathered up a few and presented them for us to gaze upon. But they are, after all, but few in comparison with those which remain ungathered; and we must wait the day when we shall hear the whole glorious history of that wondrous life, and have fact upon fact presented to us, and word upon word — all detailed to us in blessed profusion and endless number, either from the lips of His disciples, or better still, from His own. The full detail of these will of itself be enough to fill up the days and nights of eternity.

But though by far the greater number of His words and deeds is left unrecorded, enough has been preserved to answer the divine purpose with us here. Nay, we may say that this abstract or abridgment of His life, this culling from the events of that life, is far better for us than a larger history would have been. We should but have been bewildered, distracted, with more; and though we have often said to ourselves, and to one another, 'Would that we knew more of the Lord's life!' we knew not what we said. The gratification of such a wish just now would not be for the better to us, but for the worse. All that we need has been retained for our use here, and we are quite sure that the rest are not thrown away. They jewels are too precious to be lost. They are but treasured up for future use, to be brought forth to us hereafter. For we are not done knowing Christ when we see Him face to face. We shall only have begun.

Had this abridgment or selection been a *human* one, we might have been somewhat stumbled. We might have asked, Is it a fair one? Does it give a proper view of the case? Does it place the evidence upon its proper basis, and bring out all its strength? But knowing that it is a *divine*, not *human* selection, we have no such questions to ask. The selection of facts and words must be perfect of its kind, misrepresenting nothing, neither understating nor overstating anything; giving us such a sketch of the earthly life of the Christ as would produce the true impression, the exact feeling or state of mind, which would have been produced had the whole been presented to us, and had we been able to grasp, or weight, or comprehend that whole. It is the Holy Spirit who has abridged for us the life of the Son of God; and that abridgment must not only be thoroughly accurate, but so adjusted and balanced in all its part as to do its work most efficiently, to present the evidence most strongly; to strengthen, not to weaken, the intended impression; to concentrate, not to diffuse or dilute the light.

Hence it is that apostle, while reminding us of many *unrevealed* signs, adds this regarding the *recorded* ones: 'These are written, that ye might believe that Jesus is the Christ, the Son of God.' We take the recorded signs as so many divine messages to us, so many heavenly rays converging on the person of Jesus of Nazareth; and we take them, too, as specimens of the *unrecorded* — each miracle a representative of multitudes of unrecorded miracles, each word a representative of millions of unrecorded words. We thus learn that while much has been left ungathered, yet that which is left is of the same tenor with that which has been preserved: the unknown does not contradict the known. The evidence remaining unproduced is all in the same direction, adding to the proof that Jesus of Nazareth is all that He professed to be.

These signs are worth the studying. They are full of meaning. Each one is big with everlasting truth, with divine and infinite love.

2. The Faith — The faith had its root in the 'signs' or in the divine statement concerning the signs; for faith cometh by hearing concerning the signs; for faith cometh by hearing, and hearing by the word of God. The signs were especially wrought for the production of this faith, and they are selected and recorded for the same purpose to us. They are the foundation of faith, not simply as miracles, but as miracles of a certain kind, and with a definite bearing. Their *meaning* is unambiguous. They have one voice and one object. They all bear upon the person and mission of Jesus of Nazareth. They speak out the mind of God concerning Him, leaving us in no doubt as to this point — what God thinks of Him.

   These signs, though having one voice and one meaning, bear upon our faith in a threefold way.

   (1.) They testify that Jesus of Nazareth is the Sent of God — As Nicodemus declared, 'No man can do these miracles except God be with him.' This was the point to which Jesus brought the Pharisees: either these

miracles are God's doing or Satan's, and prove that I am sent either of God or of Satan. But all these miracles are all *against* Satan and for God, as well as for the good of man; they must be of divine origin, and prove me to be sent of God. 'I came from God', He said, and these works are the proof that this is true.

(2.) They testify that Jesus is the Christ — the miracles were not merely great, but *peculiar*; just such miracles as the prophets had predicted that Messiah, when He came should perform. Hence, when John's disciples came with the question, 'Art thou He who should come? Jesus 'in that same hour,' and before their eyes, wrought certain miracles, and sent back the messengers to John with this message from Himself. 'Go and show John again those things which ye do hear and see: the blind receive their sight, and the lame walk; the lepers are cleansed, and the deaf hear; the dead are raised up, and the poor have the gospel preached to them' (Matt. 11:4-5). These were the signs which were to satisfy John and his disciples that Jesus was the Christ of God, the Messiah of the prophets, the seed of the woman who had come to bruise the serpent's head, and to destroy the works of the devil.

(3.) *They testify that Jesus is the Son of God* — If He were Messiah, then, by inference, He was known to be the Son of God. But some of His 'signs' went more directly to prove the Sonship, especially the resurrection. By this, says the apostle, He was 'declared to be the Son of God with power.' It was as the Son that He had so often spoken in the Psalms concerning His own resurrection by his Father's power, and as the fruit of the Father's love. 'Thou wilt not leave my soul in hell, neither wilt Thou suffer Thine Holy One to see corruption.' And when proving to Thomas that He was in very deed the crucified Jesus, who was dead and was alive again, He was proving that He was the Son of God, He of whom it had been said, 'Thou art my Son, this day have I begotten Thee.'

Thus, then, these divinely selected and divinely recorded signs bear upon the person of Christ in these three points: they declare Him to be the Sent of God, to be the Christ of God, to be the Son of God. And under these three heads, all that we need to know of Him is comprised. These signs have no meaning, if they do not mean these three things; and if they do mean these things, then what excuse have we for unbelief? What a perfect foundation have we for faith in Him! How can we but believe? 'These are written, that we might believe that Jesus is the Christ, the Son of God.' And in the day of weariness and doubt, let us ever fall back on these to renew and confirm us. Let us not delude ourselves with the idea that we are only '*doubting ourselves*,' or doubting our own faith, and not doubting what God has recorded. Unbelief is a far deeper and deadlier thing than merely doubting *ourselves*. No man ever dishonored Christ or flung away his soul by doubting *himself*. The evil is, that at such times we really doubt the very simplest truths of Christianity, and we deceive ourselves, and soothe our consciences with the idea that we are doubting ourselves, not God, not His testimony, not Christ, not the signs concerning Him. He who has gone into the doubtings, and been, by the mercy of God, removed from them, will be the first to acknowledge that his doubts were, when analyzed, of a far deadlier nature than he had at first supposed them; that they really struck at the very truth of God, and that in all these doubts he discovered not only the manifestations of self-righteousness, but the indications of atheism. He thought at first that he was humbly siding with God against his own evil self, but soon he saw that he was siding with self and with the devil against God and His truth. He was actually rejecting the testimony of the Father concerning the Son. He was refusing either to believe the signs, or to interrupt them aright. The secret thought of the doubting heart, under whatever disguises it may cloak itself, is that Jesus of Nazareth is not the Christ, nor the Son of God.

3. *The Life* – the faith which roots itself in these signs is connected with *life*. We believe, and we live. 'Faith is the substance of things hoped for, the evidence of things not seen.' And when faith is connected with the Christ, then the unseen thing which it finds in Him is *life*. He that believeth on the Son hath everlasting life.'

It is not easy to define 'life,' but we may say that it consists in such things as these: (1) Forgiveness, or deliverance from condemnation; for condemnation is death, and the life which we get from Christ is the reversal of this death: 'Through this man is preached unto us the forgiveness of sins; there is no condemnation to them that are in Christ Jesus.' (2) The possession of that new being or nature by which is I Am; that Christ who is the life; that last Adam, who is not only a 'living soul,' but a 'quickening Spirit.' (3) Replenishment with holiness; for as unholiness is death, and death is unholiness, so holiness is life, and life is holiness. The sinner exists, but does not live; the saint lives as well as exists. (4) Participation of all happiness. Life is not life without joy. Joy is like the blood of the body. Exhaust the blood, the man's life is gone. So drain the soul of joy, and all that deserves the name of life has fled. It is not so unimportant or unessential a thing to be happy as some men tell us. Happiness is the very essence of true life; and hence, Jesus comes to us with rest, peace, and joy at the very outset. 'These things I have spoken unto you, that my joy might be full.' Christ's own joy in its fullness is then the very life of life. (5) Hope of resurrection, or rather we should say, resurrection itself. For in Christ we have such a pledge of resurrection, that we may be said to be already risen, already possessed of our resurrection bodies. 'When Christ who is our life shall appear, we shall appear with Him in glory;' meanwhile, until He appeareth, we may reckon ourselves possessed of the glory and the life, even in the midst of the shame and death of this present evil world.

All things are comprised in the 'life' of which our text speaks. Life is not merely salvation, or deliverance from the eternal woe. It includes these, but it rises far beyond them. It is the reversal of all that the first Adam brought on his sons by his transgression; it is the bestowment of the fullness of the last Adam upon us, making us one with Him who is our life, making us partakers of the divine nature, filling us not merely with the life of angels, or the life of heaven, but with the life of the Son of God. His life is ours; because He liveth, we live also. Our life is hidden with Christ in God.

The link, the one link, between us and this life is faith. Believing, we have life. It is the link between us and the life, because it is the link between us and Christ. Life is the result of connection with Christ Himself.

In days of His miracles here on earth, contact with Him was everything. In some cases it was the sick man's touch of Him, in others it was His touch of the sick man that accomplished the healing. Both ways are recorded, that we may see that the contact is mutual; that the great thing, the one thing, is *contact*, whether that be our touching Him, or His touching us. Just as sometimes He is spoken of as coming to us, and at other times we are spoken of as coming to Him. Herein is reference to the touch. He is said to touch us, we to touch Him. In both cases it is personal and direct and contact with Him. Nothing else will do.

There must be connection with the Christ, the Son of God — not connection with a creed, or a catechism, or a church, or a minister, or a godly ancestry, but with Christ Himself. It is this that saves, and everything that falls short of this fails to win the life. Pardon, peace, rest, life — all that a sinner needs is to be thus obtained. There is no other way. Prayers, tears, almsdeeds, mortification, penance, toil, suffering, religious performances all are vain. Only in contact with the living Christ is there life for the dead in sin.

It is the Holy Spirit's work to bring about this vital contact. It is He who takes the dead soul and connects it with the source of life. Flesh and blood could not accomplish this; would never think of this; would not wish it; nay, would resist it to the uttermost. Yes, it requires the almightiness of God to effect a result so utterly opposed to, and so strenuously resisted by, feeling of the natural man.

But while the work and the Agent are supernatural, the way is natural. The Holy Spirit 'worketh faith in us, and thereby uniteth us to Christ.' He opens our eyes

to see the signs done by Jesus, and to understand the truth connected with these. When thus brought to recognize in Jesus, Him whom the Father had sent into the world as the life of men, the Way, the Truth, and the Life, the connection between us and the source of life is established. Life flows into us — His life — the life which quickens the dead, the life which makes us fit for the kingdom of life.

'Believing,' we *have* life! Whether we may be recognizing it or not, we *have* it; for the word of God is sure, and the life is connected not with *feeling,* but with *faith.*

'Believing,' we *have* life! However unlike the living we may be, however burdened, and feeble, and dark, we *have* life; for God hath given His sure word of promise.

Having life, we walk, and work, and act, and speak as living men. We go forward in joy, and liberty, and vigour to do the work of Him who hath quickened us. We start upon the race for us, not darkly nor uncertainly, but as men who know their calling, and have their eye distinctly upon the goal.

4. *The Name* — in Scripture, the name of a person has a twofold reference. (1) It distinguishes the individual from all others; (2) It expresses his character. So the name of God, 'Jehovah,' marks Him out of all other gods, and also indicates His character, 'the Lord God, merciful and gracious.' So the name or names of Christ both single Him out and intimate His nature, His character, His work — Jesus, Immanuel, Christ, the Lord, the Lamb.

Through these, as it were, the life flows out from Him to us. They are the fountains to which we apply our thirsty lips and drink of the water of life. For each of them pours a gushing stream of immortality.

The use of the singular number here, and often elsewhere ('name,' not 'names'), implies, however, something more than this. 'Name' is no doubt' the gathering together or concentration the others into *one*. But there is more in the word than this. The name of a person is often used as equivalent to the authority or power of that person; so when I use his name, all his influence passes over to me, and I get all that he would be entitled to obtain. In order to get the full meaning of our text, we must add this last idea to the former. Thus, in Acts

3:16, 'His name, through faith in His name, hath made this man strong.'

In this the name of Christ is 'a power' — something potential, influential, omnipotent — that our text speaks of. It is not only the name of names. It not only contains in itself that truth and love which, when believed, quicken the soul; but it is all-prevailing, when made use of by the sinner with God in order to obtain life.

The *name is mighty*. It can command. It speaks with authority. He that uses it may reckon on receiving what he needs. 'Concerning the works of my hands command ye me.' Thus we go to God, employing this omnipotent name.

This name is of great price. It can purchase life and all things that we need. He who makes use of this name in his heavenly commerce is sure to prosper. Going with it into market, he can purchase anything. There is nothing in all the stores of God which is too precious to be bought by gold.

Especially, however, in obtaining *life*, is this name to be used. Having learned who Jesus really is and having discovered in Him the Christ, the Son of God, we say: Ah, then, His name is all we need. It must be sufficient to obtain life for us. And thus going to God, we get life 'through His name.' Life in Christ! Life from Christ! Life through His name! This is the sum of our message. It is glad tidings of great joy. We proclaim aloud this *name*. We tell its virtues, its power, its preciousness, its sufficiency. We present it to each of you for present use. God bids you to use it. It is just the name you need. He bids you come to Him with it, and you are sure to succeed, on whatsoever errand you come. Nothing can withstand it. Nothing is too excellent to be beyond its power to purchase. Only credit what God tells you of it. Take it at once; use it as those who know that God would not deceive you in such a matter, nor put a false value on the name of His Son.

Life through the name of Jesus! Listen, ye dead in sin. Hear, and your souls shall live. There is no other name possessed of virtue or value equal to this. Honor this excellent name by using it; show that the value which *you* set upon it is the same that *God* does by going to Him with it, to purchase from Him the life which a sinner needs.

Do not undervalue that name, nor discredit the divine testimony to its potency. Do not mistrust it when you go to God with it; but act with the confidence — the reverent confidence — of a man who is assured that that name is all that has been said; nay, that the half has not been told him concerning its power and value. Mix nothing with it; add nothing to it; nothing of self, nothing of man, nothing either of earth or heaven. Take it as it is — alone, perfect, all powerful. You cannot trust it too much, nor expect too great things from your employment of it in the transactions between you and God.

CHAPTER 9

ABIDING IN THE SON AND IN THE FATHER

The Lord's own words in the gospel of John are remarkable for their references to our connection with the Christ, as that of being *in Him* and abiding in Him; of being in the truth, and abiding in the truth.

The bearing of all the following remarks upon this, and this upon the proceeding remarks, will be obvious. Connection with the Christ of God in most intimate closeness is that which is affirmed to be the beginning, middle, and end of a Christian man's life on earth. This connection is brought about through the truth by the power of the Holy Ghost; and the exhortations, as well as warnings respecting all this, are the most solemn, and I might add, vehemently kind.

Let us, for the enforcement of this, take up more especially and in detail one verse, 1 John 2:24. The whole of this Epistle bears more or less directly upon these points; but this verse brings them home to the Christian's conscience, and refers to their lifelong application to the Christian's walk with God.

The word 'you' is in the Greek, emphatic from its position and its construction. The apostle is writing to men exposed to seducing influences; tempted with perilous error; and assailed by 'many antichrists.' 'Whatever others may think or do, however far they may go astray or blaspheme — do *you* hold fast that which ye have received?' This was his earnest message to the saints of the first century; it is no less his exhortation and his warning to the Church of the nineteenth.

It is of 'the truth' (ver. 21) that he is speaking; he gives it a special name, 'that which they had heard from the beginning;' he beseeches them to let that truth abide; he announces the blessed results of so doing.

1. *The Truth* — both in his Gospel and in his Epistles he dwells on what he calls by preeminence THE TRUTH, and lays great stress on the things that are TRUE: the *true* words and the *true* facts. He relates, too, the Master's allusions to Himself as 'the truth;' (John 8:45)' and he takes special pains to inform us that his own record is true, and that he knows it is true; and all this to furnish a firm foundation for our faith: 'He that saw it bare record, and his record is *true*, and he knoweth that he saith *true*, that ye might believe' (John 19:35). The Master had said — 'My record is *true*; My judg-

ment is true;' 'If I say the *truth*, why do ye not believe me?' On *true* things, *true* words, a *true* person, and a *true* history, John would have us rest our faith; not on opinion, or speculation, or reasoning, but on evidence of the surest kind, the testimony of honest witnesses; on that which is more satisfying and immovable than human demonstration, the testimony of the God who cannot lie. Thus, he teaches us to say in regard to divine things, 'we *know* them;' not we think or conjecture, but we *know*; they are absolutely true and certain; and our belief of them rests on the explicit word of God. Our faith rises above all other faith, not because it is of superior quality in itself, but because it rests on a divine basis — the authority of the God of truth. This is the immovable rock on which we rest; a rock which time and age cannot crumble down; a rock against which waves rush and winds roar in vain. O rock of God, rock of ages, rock of eternity, how firm the faith, how blessed the man, that rests on Thee!

2. *The name by which he here designates the Truth* — 'That which ye have heard from the beginning;' an expression very like one of the Master's, when He said to the Jews, 'Even the same that I said unto you from the beginning.' The truth, then, of which John spoke to them was not *new*, but *old*. It was the one unvarying thing which they had all along heard: not modified, or improved upon, or refined, so as to suit the times; but the same, unchanged and unchangeable. When

apostles came amongst them for the first time, they preached 'the word of THE TRUTH of the gospel;' and in that word, that truth, that gospel, there had been no improvements; nothing had become obsolete, and nothing required amendment. That which they had heard from the beginning was all that they were called to abide on now. Nothing needed to be added to, or taken from it. Its contents were infinitely varied; but it remained ever the same.

In this respect it is like the works of God's hand around us. There is the sun in the firmament, just the same as at the beginning, in form, motion, light, and heat. It has not begun to be reckoned obsolete; nor has something new been proposed as a substitute. It does not require improvement; men have not begun to weary of it; nor have flaws been discovered in its glorious radiance. Development, in the sense of drawing out its treasures, and unfolding its beauties and perfections, is proceeding as science expands; but development in the sense of addition, or improvement, is not dreamt of even as a possibility. Men are content with their old sun; the sun of Adam, the sun of Noah, the sun of Moses, and Joshua, the sun that was lighted up on the fourth day; the sun that rose over Sodom, the sun that stood still on Gibeon; the sun that was darkened for three hours at Jerusalem and over all the land. Modern enlightenment has not yet affirmed that its theories of progress admit of application to the sun, or that a higher science may yet do for astronomy what a higher criticism and a more advanced theology are doing for religious truth, and for 'the Christ of God.'

That which we have heard from the beginning is the same that we are to hear and obey now; for the truth is like the true One Himself — the same yesterday, and today, and forever. And like as the sun in the firmament is still the same full source of light, and heat, and fruitfulness, so is the Christ of God still, as in the ages past, the fountainhead of life, and health, and gladness. Earth is not weary of her sun; so let not the church be weary of hers. The light of the world eighteen centuries ago is the light of the world still. Truth never grows old. On her brow there are no wrinkles and no grey hairs upon her head. She does not totter with age, nor does her tongue stammer. She knows no second childhood; for she is always young, yet always ancient as well; unchanging amid changes, immortal in a land of death; perfect amid imperfection, and weakness, and decay.

But what is it that we have heard from the beginning? We have heard that the Word was made flesh; that God so loved the world as to give His Son. We have heard that God is love, that the cross of Christ is the exponent of that love, and the exhibition of the righteousness in conjunction with which that love has come to us. We have heard of the precious blood of Christ as cleansing, reconciling, healing and comforting. We have heard of the eternal life which has come to us as God's free gift through the death of the Prince of Life. We have heard of the record of testimony concerning this life which God has proclaimed. We have heard of the Advocate with the Father, Jesus Christ, the righteous. We have heard of the divine generosity that has made us sons of God, heirs of God, and joint-heirs with Christ Jesus. We have heard of the promise of His appearing in His glory, bringing with Him resurrection, and glory, and the incorruptible inheritance. These are some of the things which we have heard from the beginning; and in hearing of which we believed, and in believing became sons and heirs.

These things have not changed nor grown obsolete. They have proved their excellency through the ages and passed through many a trial, many a scrutiny. They have resisted triumphantly the assaults of skepticism and superstition, paganism persecuted, popery veiled, rationalism undermined. But all in vain. The well is too deep for man's appliances to fill up, too clear for man's hostility to disturb, too perennial for man's anger to dry up. The living water in it is as transparent as at the first. It quenches man's thirst as thoroughly in these last days as it did in ages past. It is still a well of water springing up into everlasting life.

Most venerable name, 'that which we have heard from the beginning;' is even more venerable now than in the days of the apostle; and it is becoming more venerable every day! We need and we desire no new gospel, no new truth, as if ancient truth had become antiquated. That which gladdened the sinners of Jerusalem, or Corinth, or Ephesus, or Philippi, can gladden us still. That which fed the Church of God in primitive times can feed us in these last days. Can we ask for anything better, truer, more suited to our condition than that which the Church has heard, and which apostles preached from the beginning?

3. *The necessity for the continuance of the truth* – we may see this from what we have already said, but much more might be added to encore the apostle's exhortation. There is no other truth to substitute for it; and besides, the old is better. No second revelation has descended to us. God has not broken silence since the day He spoke in Patmos. Any new revelation must be a human one; and a human one must be infinitely inferior to the divine. It is not merely continuance in truth, but in 'the truth;' nor the continuance of the truth, but the continuance of that truth *in us*; the truth in us, and we in it so 'that which we have heard from the beginning' shall penetrate us in all its integrity and unmixed purity, pervading every part or our being, molding us, quickening us, sanctifying us, remaining with us to the end. The abiding of this truth in us, here inculcated, is broadly opposed to the flippant and superficial tenure of it by many in our day. The truth

must not lie upon the surface, like water on the rock, it must *sink* deep into us; it must not be held with levity or in sport, nor dallied with as a thing of pastime; it must be grasped in earnest, as if part of our very soul. It must not come and go, by fits and starts, for convenience, or for gain, or for approbation; it must *abide*, unchangeable, not indeed like the rock, immovable and uncommunicative, but like the river, ever flowing in its old and happy channel, diffusing fruitfulness and verdure all around.

The nonabiding of this truth in us is the cause of much that is false, hollow, and feverish in the religion of multitudes. True religion must rest upon the truth, upon 'that which we have heard from the beginning.' Truth and religion have too often been separated; and we find on the one hand truth professed without religion, and on the other hand professed without truth. Indeed, as to the latter, it is beginning to be affirmed that a man may be very religious without holding the truth, and that it is the highest form of religion that soars above creeds and doctrines, and repudiates all theologies whatever. The current of public opinion runs strongly in favor of this idea, and it is promulgated as one of the discoveries of the age, that the religious sentiment is quite independent of doctrine, and can root itself in a negation or a falsehood as naturally and properly as in a truth or a positive creed. If the Bible is to be credited, this is simply and nakedly an impossibility. The 'religious sentiment' is nothing but a fancy, or a dream, or a flight of poetry, if not the offspring of truth. We may say more: the religious sentiment, either undirected or misdirected, either under no guidance of truth or under the guidance of positive error, must be identical with idolatry or blasphemy. The Bible acknowledges no God but Jehovah, and every deviation from the right knowledge and right worship of Him is a crime. It recognizes no religion but one, founded on that which we have heard from the beginning. The religious 'sentiment' may be very fervent in the worshippers of Baal, or Jupiter, or Mary, but its fervor finds no acceptance with Him who is jealous for His name, to whom there is but one truth and one religion; who has never consented to recognize falsehood concerning Himself as an equivalent for truth regarding Himself; nor man's ideas of what God should be as a substitute for what He declares that God is, nor the shifting theories of religion as equally good, equally safe, and equally satisfactory with 'that which we have heard from the beginning.'

4. *The Results* — 'Ye also shall continue in the Father and in the Son.' There is certainly something wonderful and glorious here. There is another side of divine truth presented to us, and another view of our relationship to God. The result of abiding in the truth will be abiding in the Father and the Son; and, of course, departure from that truth will be expulsion

or estrangement from the Father and the Son. The beginning of our religion was coming to the Father, and this we did in believing the truth upon His own testimony. The continuance of our religion was an abiding in the Father, and this through abiding in the truth. So with regard to the Son: we came to be in Him; and as we began, so we carry on; that which we heard from the beginning remains in us; and so we remain in the Father and the Son. Rejection of the truth involves the loss of this position, this relationship; and the more of divine truth that we possess, the more is this position confirmed, and the more fully does this relationship develop itself.

But what is meant by 'continuing in the Father and the Son'? It is not enough to say that it means continuing to know, or continuing to have fellowship with, or continuing to worship, or continuing to love and be loved. It implies something deeper, more intimate, more full than this. The figure is taken first of all from our Lord's own discourses. 'At that day ye shall know that I am in my Father, and ye in me, and I in you.' 'Abide in me, and I in you: as the branch cannot bear fruit of itself, except it abide in the vine, no more can ye, except ye abide in me,' The connection between our abiding in Him and the truth abiding in us is also affirmed by our Lord: 'If a man love me, he will keep my words; and my Father will love him, and we will come unto him, and make our abode with him;' and again, 'If ye abide in me, and my words abide in you.'

(1.) We are in the Father and the Son, as the Father Himself is in the Son, and the Son in the Father (John 17:21). Nothing can imply *intimacy* more fully than this.

(2.) We are in the Father and in the Son as the seed is in the soil, or as the graft is in the branch. This is intimacy proceeding fruitfulness, and furnishing us with sap and life — intimacy growing into perfect oneness.

(3.) We are in the Father and Son as the inmate of a house is within its walls, surrounded by it on all sides for shelter, comfort, and all the joys of home. This home intimacy is as close as can be conceived, he who enjoys it being compassed about with divine light, and love, and glory.

(4.) We are in the Father and in the Son as the gold and silver are in the treasure-house, and as the treasure house itself is in the fortress, doubly surrounded, for completeness of safety. 'Our life is hid with Christ of God.'

(5.) We are in the Father and in the Son as was Jerusalem in the midst of the encircling hills. 'As the mountains are round about Jerusalem, so the Lord is round His people, from henceforth ever forever.' What absolute security and repose does this imply! The Father and the Son our walls and bulwarks!

(6.) We are in the Father and in the Son as was the manna in the ark of the covenant, safe in the very holies; or as the pillar spoken of in the promise to the Philadelphian church: 'Him that overcometh will I make a pillar in the temple of my God, and he shall go no more out;' the ornament and glory of the eternal house in which the redeemed shall dwell and worship forever.

These may be taken as parts of the figure here made use of, insofar as it is figure; but the fullness of the blessing, and honor, and joy, and security, and light, here shadowed forth, no human lip or pen can set forth. We cannot know it rightly now, but we shall know it hereafter; only there seems something so unutterably glorious and blessed in the thought, that we might almost say, we shall never fully understand the mystery. But God, our God, understands it fully, and He can and will give us the full benefit of it, whether we understand it or not. Out of these half-understood expressions, He can enable us to draw unceasing gladness and holiness, unfolding to us in His own way and time more and more of their unsearchable riches; and through 'that which we have heard from the beginning,' making us each day more abundantly partakers of His fellowship through the indwelling of the Holy Ghost.

CHAPTER 10

THE FUTURE GLORY OF THE CHRIST

Earth has a future in connection with the Christ of God. His body is composed of its dust, and this of itself forms a link which cannot be broken.

The Son of God is the 'second man,' or 'last Adam,' and as such He is to have dominion over all that of which the first Adam was king. God's eternal purpose includes not only the king, but the kingdom; and the history of the Christ carries along with it the history of this earth, past, present, and to come.

We have already alluded to this passing; but before we close, let us take it up a little more fully; and let us do so in connection with the second chapter of the Epistle to the Hebrews, where the humiliation and the glory of 'the Christ' are brought strikingly into view. Without expounding that chapter in detail, we may bring out some of its more outstanding points.

Into four great parts, or sections, does the apostle here divide the history of Him who is the brightness of Jehovah's glory and the express image of His person. Of these sections the headings are these: the things which we have seen, or Jesus made a little lower than the angels; the things which we do not see (*i.e.*, which do not yet exist), all things that we do see (i.e. which now exist), or Jesus crowned with glory and honor; the things that we shall see, or all things put in subjection under Him, and the kingdoms of earth made His *de facto*, as they have been His *de jure*, from the beginning. Each of these four points the apostle brings to bear upon his argument, in his great demonstration of the super Adamic, super Angelic, super Mosaic, glory of the Christ, the last Adam, the Head, the King, the Priest of 'the world to come.'

The first two of these four parts are marked by a common aspect of darkness; the second two, by a common aspect of brightness. The first of all is the period of Messiah's self-abnegation here, in the days of His flesh, when though rich, for our sakes He became poor, was made perfect through sufferings, and bore our curse upon the tree. The second is the present period of His non-manifestation and non-assumption of actual and visible rule in our world, to which as the risen Christ and the enthroned King He was entitled, but for which He was content to wait for the fullness of the times, and the gradual evolution of the Father's eternal purpose. The third is the period of His investiture with the royalty of heaven. His session on the Father's throne; angels and authorities, and powers are being made subject unto Him. The fourth is the period of His manifestation or glory here, when His enemies shall be made His footstool, and all things put under Him, when, as the 'second man,' He shall undo what the 'first man' did; and as Son of God, yet also Son of Mary, Son of David, Son of Abraham, Son of Adam, Seed of the woman, true Heir of all things, He shall gather up unto Himself the unfinished types, predictions, and foreshadows, in which the Church of past ages dimly saw Him, and in the name of the humanity which He represents, dispossess the usurper, and claim creations for His own.

The *first* of these four epochs has long since run its course, and the *last* has not yet begun; but the *second* and the *third* are now in progress. The things which we do not see, and the things which we do see, are now unfolding themselves, parallel and contemporaneous with each other; the one in heaven, the other upon earth; the one all obedience, and splendor, and holiness, the other all rebellion, and shadow, and sin — like a sky of sunshine bending over a wild and lawless ocean; or like two streams, one clear, the other turbid, flowing separate, yet parallel, and terminating in a clear, calm lake, in which the one loses all its foulness, and into which the other pours all it translucent crystal.

It is at this interval that we stand; realizing both the evil and the good — the evil all around us, and the good above us — and longing for the time when the light shall descend and swallow up the darkness; when the terrestrial shall take on the image of the celestial; when neither the moral nor the physical world shall be 'without form and void;' when obedience shall take the place of rebellion, and instead of the multitude of warring wills, the one will shall be done on earth as it is done in heaven.

Seeing Jesus now crowned with glory and honor, yet not seeing all things put under Him, but the world lying in wickedness — the lawless on giving law to the nations, and Satan inspiring the false religions of earth — we should feel like disappointed men, and be tempted to ask, 'Where is the promise of His coming?' Did we not remember that the Church's posture in the Bridegroom's absence is that of patient waiting; and that it is God Himself who has taught us this song of hope: 'Let the heavens rejoice, and let the earth be glad; let the field be joyful, and all that is therein; let the floods clap their hands; let the hills be joyful together before the Lord; for He cometh, for He cometh to judge the earth.'

The apostle designates this interval or break by the word 'Now' — *Now* we see not yet all things put under Him, but we see Jesus crowned with glory and honor. In reference to this interval, he elsewhere uses the same word, in various aspects: 'Christ is not entered into the holy places made with hands, but into heaven itself, *now* to appear in the presence of God for us' (Heb. 9:24). 'Behold, *now* is the accepted time; behold, *now* is the day of salvation' (2 Cor. 6:2). 'The whole creation groaneth and travaileth in pain together until now' (Rom. 8:22). 'The spirit that *now* worketh in the children of disobedience' (Eph. 2:2). 'Even *now* are there many antichrists'

(1 John 2:18). Of the *length* of this 'now,' little is said; but of its bearings on us, and of its momentous character as the womb of infinite events and eternal issues, much has been written by the Spirit of God. Again and again, for warning, persuasion, instruction, consolation, He has held up to us this interval, so unique in its character, and so marvelous in its results; and he has made that word 'now' to ring in our ears.

An interval so long and gloomy, filled up during so many centuries with revolt, and defiance, and blasphemy, is not what we should have expected. Seeing that all power, on earth as well as in heaven, was given Him as the risen Christ; seeing that He fought the fight, and won the victory upon the cross; we wonder that He should not at once reap the harvest; that He should still be rejected of men, His Church a minority, His cause upon the losing side, Himself defied by that world which He overcame, that Satan whom He led captive, that death over which He triumphed, that curse, for the enduring of which He took flesh and died.

Under this sore perplexity and disappointment we take refuge where *He* did, when men turned away from His words: 'Even so, Father, for so it seemed good in Thy sight.' The purpose of God, as we read it in the light of ages, assumes the necessity for the development of evil, and error, and unbelief, and rebellion; so as to bring out, not merely what the fall did, the frailty of creaturehood, but the depths of Satan and the depths of sin — the abysses of evil that are to be found in every corner of a human heart. In the sight of

God, this development of creature fallibility and evil is a thing of vast moment, and has a far larger space assigned to it in the history of men and devils than our philosophy would deem safe, or our theology account for. The revelation of evil upon earth before Messiah came was fearful; but it was explicable on the fact that the Destroyer of evil had not yet descended. But its far wider range and more malignant type since He came, nay since He finished His sin-bearing work; nay since He sat down upon the throne, are more perplexing, and no less appalling. Terrible are these words of His, 'I came not to send peace upon earth, but a sword.'

O sin, what an infinite evil art thou! How exceeding sinful, and how prolific in thy sinfulness; how tenacious of life; how expansive in thy potency; how remorseless in thy cruelty; how all-pervading in thy dominion over creaturehood; one seed of thine, dropped on Paradise, covering earth for six thousand years with its hellish harvest! O heart of man, what a pit, what a sea of wickedness, and lawlessness, and atheism art thou! O Satan, god of this world, and ruler of its darkness, how vast thy resources of strength, and skill, and cunning; defeated, yet gathering power from defeat; wounded with a deadly wound eighteen hundred years ago, yet still surviving, and mustering thy hosts for battle: still multiplying thy subtle wiles, and seducing sophistries, and strong delusions, and dazzling falsehoods, to deceive if possible the very elect; still forging thy fiery darts and wounding men to death, or leading them captive at will; still warring against truth, hiding the gospel, raging against the Lamb, assailing His cross, His throne, and His saints; still vitalizing the old and sapless idolatries of earth, inventing new infidelities, sending forth new blasphemies, making not heathendom, nor Moslemdom, but Christendom, thy chief seat and chosen citadel; and exercising a power everywhere that both alarms and perplexes us, as if the Christ of God had not been really crowned, or as if the reins of the universe had snapped asunder in His hands!

This is then the fact to which we ask your attention, 'Now we see not yet all things put under Him.'

The word translated 'put under' does not merely intimate abstract right, but actual surrender and obedience. That Christ is Prince of the kings of the earth, and Head over all things, as well as Head of His body the Church, is part of every Christian creed; but to how few — individuals churches, nations — is it aught beyond a mere abstraction! The recognition of the dogma is accompanied with no acknowledgement of the laws in which it declares itself, and with no subjection, personal, political, or ecclesiastical, to Him for whom the Father claims absolute obedience: 'Kiss ye the Son.'

The abstract right or prerogative is that which the apostle demonstrates from the eighth psalm: 'Unto the angels hath He not put in subjection the world to come, whereof we speak; but one is a certain place testified, saying, What is *man*, that Thou art mindful of him? Or the son of man, that Thou visitest him? Thou madest him a little lower than the angels; thou crownest him with glory and honor, and didst set him over the work of Thy hands.' Thus this psalm, which carries us back to the first chapter of Genesis, and embodies God's original grant of authority over creation to the *first* Adam, is accepted by the apostle as a proof of God's purpose to confer on Christ, as the *last* Adam, the lapsed sovereignty and forfeited sceptre of the *first*; to perpetuate in the line and dynasty of that race which Adam represented the lordship of His handiwork; not to alienate the inheritance because of the transgression of the first proprietor, but to continue it in the same stock and family; to place, not upon an angelic, but a human brow, creation's diadem; to confide, not to angelic, but to human hands, the sceptre of the universe.

The apostle shows this grant of dominion to the last Adam to be as wide as God's creation, For thus he interrupts and expands the psalmist's words, 'in that He put all in subjection under Him, He left nothing that is not put under Him.' So that as in *person* the last Adam is more glorious than the first, so is His throne more exalted, and His empire as much larger in compass, as is His worthiness of honor and fitness to reign. In Him, as very God and very man, the crowns of heaven and earth are united; and the slain Lamb is He who alone is worthy to receive power, and riches, and wisdom, and honor, and glory, and blessing, from every creature in heaven, and earth, and sea.

What then? Has God's purpose failed or changed? Has the rebellion of this present evil world proved stronger than was reckoned on? For the right of dominion and the actual subjection have not been co-extensive. Christ is King of kings, yet Satan is still god of this world, and prince of the power of the air. It is to this point of divergency between the earthly and the heavenly, of conflict between the rightful and the actual, that the apostle brings us when he says, 'But now we see not yet all things put under Him;' just as our Lord Himself did in the parable of the nobleman who went in to the far country, to receive for himself a kingdom, and to return; but who, in the interval of absence, was but poorly served by some of his servants, and hated by his citizens. The divine meaning of this strange divergency between the upper and lower regions of Messiah's domain is too large and too profound a subject for present discussion. The reasons for this delay in assimilating the terrestrial to the celestial; in transmuting the universal *right* into the universal *fact;* in following up the conferred *sovereignty* with the accomplished *submission*, would lead us into the mystery of sin's first entrance and present sufferance, as well as into the question why a sinner at his conversion is not at once made perfect, and not at once translated into the heavenly glory. Our subject is simply to call attention to the state of *non-submission to Christ* in which we find our world, and which is declared to be especially the characteristic of the interval, or 'now,' spoken of by Paul. Man and his world have not yet bent the knee to Him' and the Father has not yet interposed to bring about the submission. 'Thy people shall be willing in the day of Thy power,' is still a futurity both for Israel and for the World.

Let us look at the *facts* referred to in the words, 'We see not yet all things put under Him.'

1. Christ is a Savior; yet all have not been saved. His *power* to deliver is as boundless as His right is unchangeable; yet millions have perished since He ascended the throne, All have not come, and the Father has not drawn them. Few are saved; many are called, but few are chosen. Messiah is still the rejected of men. This is *personal non-submission*, in other words, *unbelief*; individual refusal of the great salvation; the soul's deliberate rejection of God's free gift of everlasting life; the sinner's determination not to submit himself to the righteousness of God.

Hear yon reckless scoffer, as he says, I want none of your Christs or your pardons, your gospels or your Bibles. I care not for your heaven, and do not fear your hell, or your devil, or your judgment day. Hear yon proud Unitarian, as he tells you, I believe not in your Trinity, or your Incarnation; and I had rather risk all your hells than be so mean as to take a salvation which I had not deserved, or could not pay for: fair play and no favor is all I ask. See you poor Romanist, doting upon his penances, and throwing them into the scale with the sufferings of the Son of God. Listen to you Protestant, unpricked in conscience and whole in heart, but religious after a sort, as he congratulates himself on his good life and sound creed as his passport to the kingdom. Mark you awakened sinner, who has just made the discovery of the hell within him, crying for mercy, and asking, What must I *do* to be saved? And to whom we speak in vain of the completed propitiation of the cross. Are not all these specimens of non-submission to the Son of God — rebellion against His power as Savior of the lost? Are they not some of the many ways in which man's dissatisfaction with the cross, and his disbelief of the divine testimony to the work of the Sinbearer, give vent to themselves; in which is daily coming to pass the saying that is written, 'Now we see yet all things put under Him'?

O man, child of rebellion and wrath! Hast thou submitted thyself to the Son of God? Hast thou received the Father's testimony to Him by whom the lost are saved; and in receiving that testimony ended forever thy rebellion against Him? Is the work done upon the cross, by which God justifies the sinner, thy one resting place? And does the great salvation satisfy thee, so as to give thee God's sure peace, and introduce thee onto the liberty of happy sonship? Or art thou still an alien, a stranger, a rebel? If so, poor soul, what will thy non-submission avail thee in the day when the Father shall take righteous vengeance upon the despisers of His Son? How shalt thou escape, if thou neglectest the great salvation?

2. *Christ is Teacher*; yet the world remains untaught. He has compassion on the ignorant, but the ignorant do not avail themselves of His pity. He says, 'Learn of me;' but men refuse His instruction, and slight His wisdom. He is God's Prophet; the one infallible Master, in whose school there is no

speculation, or conjecture, or mysticism, but only truth. He teaches as One that has authority, and claims the submission of the human intellect. Hear me, says a human teacher; and everyone who has something of moment to say may claim a *hearing*. One teacher alone is entitled to say, Hear me, and *at your peril disbelieve my doctrine*. Human reason asserts itself the judge of divine revelation, and declines to receive its philosophy or its theology from any infallibility beyond itself, from any oracle beyond its own intuitions. Science proffers but scanty allegiance to this heavenly Teacher; poetry does not sing His praises; history is not woven with His name; philosophy craves no help from Him; metaphysics is often the perversion of His truth; and fiction excludes Him from its pages of sensation, and passion, and vanity. The press is not upon His side; in the great world of journalism He is hardly named; in the chairs of learning He has no seat, and often in the pulpit His truth is muffled, if not disowned. Scholars blush to name Him, critics scrutinize His words with less reverence than those of Homer or Cicero; statesmen go not to Him for counsel; the wisdom of this world refuses to own anything to Him, and its literature world counts itself disfigured by an allusion to the cross. As a new classification of human ideas, or a new exposition of social ethics, somewhat more elevated than those of Persia, or Greece, or Rome, His Gospel may be listened to, but not as the good news from heaven, in the belief of which is life, in the non-belief of which is death.

It is not merely you German pantheist turning the New Testament story into a myth; nor yon French infidel, dissolving the biography of the Son of God into a romance; nor you African dignitary, giving the broad lie to Moses and the prophets; nor you philosophic lecturer, boasting of a Christian liberality that can afford to be generous to Jupiter; nor yon bevy of poets and artists, sighing over the gods of Greece, or retouching the worn-out statues of Apollo, or re-beautifying the obsolete idolatries in their chants to Endymion and Astarte, or gilding (to speak colloquially, *whitewashing*) the obscenities of heathendom by their fair idealisms. But it is that the tone of literature, and science, and art, is not Christian. The current of the age — in the Church an *under*-current, in the world an *upper* current — is running against the Bible, and especially against the cross of Christ. The leaders of opinion refuse to be led by the one Prophet sent from God, and would rather go back to the care of the sibyl, or the grove of Dodona, than consult the Urim and the Thummim on the breastplate of God's Prophet-priest, in whom are hidden all the treasures of wisdom and knowledge. This intellectual rebellion against Christ as the divine Prophet, this philosophical non-submission to Him, indicates too plainly that all things are not yet put under Him.

Going apart, from all these insincerities and perversities, separating thyself from these philosophies, hast thou, O brother-man, delivered thyself over to the divine tuition of the great Prophet, so as to draw thy scholarship from Him? Is that truth to thee which He teaches? Is that error which He disallows? Hast thou submitted thyself, thy mind, thy soul, thy body, thy whole being, to Him? Is thy daily life the echo of His teaching? Is the business put under Him? Thy employments, thy recreations, thy pleasures, thy plans, thy expenditure, thy efforts for others, moral or physical, thy accomplishments, thy gifts, thy learning, thy speech, thy silence — are all these put under Him? Is He thy absolute Master, the Manager of thy affairs, thy Counsellor, thy Lawgiver, and thy Guide? And dost thou all the more unreservedly put what is thine under Him, because so few, in this creation of His, own either His scepter or His rod?

These are solemn words of our Prophet, 'Because I tell you the truth, ye believe me not' (John 8:45); and again, 'My sheep hear my voice, and they follow me' (John 10:27). Hast thou, O man, heard this voice, and art thou following Him who speaks? Hast thou given thyself into the hands of this great Prophet, and submitted thy whole intellectual being unreservedly to His instruction? Say not, I should in that case be a machine, a slave. Suppose it were so, would it be a misfortune to be thus moulded, irrespective of that proud will of thine, to be clay in the hands of such a potter as the Son of God? But it is not so. Never art thou more thoroughly free, more truly *thyself*, than when completely in the hands of this Prophet. For all truth is liberty, and all error bondage; and He who can give us *most* of truth is our deliverer. Call it force or compulsion, it is *divine* force, and the compulsion of Omnipotence is the perfection of creature liberty — the compulsion the irresistible light, which liberates earth each morning from the bondage of darkness, which raises the dew-drop from the cold grass, and draws it up to roam the sky in liberty and brightness; the compulsion of the hammer that smites in pieces the prisoner's chains, and *compels* him to be free!

3. *Christ is Mediator*; yet the world has not accepted His mediation. Its millions have chosen, and still choose, to stand upon their own footing, and be represented by no substitute. The communication between earth and heaven by *one divine medium* has never been recognized or acted on by men, though established and proclaimed by God. I do not refer merely to the supplanting of the One Mediatorship by that of Mary, or the saints, or the Church. I speak of man's non-acceptance of the priestly intercession of the risen Christ, in various forms, and his preference of human mediatorship, or of no mediatorship at all, to this; to stand at a distance from God is felt to be incompatible with our relation to Him as creatures, or with

our safety as sinners. There must be a *drawing near* of some kind, whether that may amount to fellowship or not; and men have multiplied inventions for securing an approach, in the idea that any method will do, if the inventor be at all in earnest. God's one way of bringing the visible into contact with the invisible, the unholy into fellowship with the holy, His one meeting place between Himself and the sinner, His one reconciliation between earth and heaven is rejected; and each man will have his own way of dealing with Jehovah. Instead of the one Priest, the one temple, the one altar, the one sacrifice, there are priests many, temples many, altars many, sacrifices without number. The one Sinbearer is not accepted; His blood, His cross, His advocacy, His intercession are treated as unimportant, if not rejected wholly.

These are blessed words of the apostle elsewhere in the same Epistle, 'Having therefore, brethren, boldness to enter into the holiest by the blood of Jesus; and having a high priest over the house of God, let us draw near with a true heart, in full assurance of faith.' In the midst of a world to whom the sacrificial mediation of Christ is nothing, shall we not cleave to the mighty privilege here presented to us? Shall we not personally realize the 'boldness' which the blood gives to each one who credits the divine testimony to its emboldening power? Or shall we treat that blood as if devoid of efficacy, and go to God in uncertainty, as men experiencing upon its properties, and incredulous of its power to purge the conscience and prevail with God?

4. *Christ is King*; yet the world has not yet honored His crown. I do not speak now of that ecclesiastical non-submission displayed by churches that name His name, yet are governed by other laws than His. I point especially to the political non-submission manifested by the kingdoms of earth. As Prince of the kings of the earth He is unrecognized, either by its princes or its people; and the thought of His royal sceptre is distasteful to kings and emperors, to presidents and statesmen. In their cabinets He has no seat assigned to Him. In their counsels, He is not consulted. They prepare their congresses, and hold their conferences, and form their conventions, without reference to Him. They enter into commercial treaties; they send out their ambassadors; they make peace or war; they construct their navies; they muster their armies; they build their fortresses; they sheathe and unsheathe their swords, without taking Him into account. We seek Him in the palace, in the castle, in the senate house, in the camp, in the fleet, in the hall of justice but we find Him not. There was room once in Bethlehem for everyone but the young Child; and there is room in this wide world for everyone but its King. Republic, monarchy, despotism, federation — they are all alike! Christ is shut out! He comes unto His own, and His own receive Him not.

Non-acceptance of the Seed of the woman as Savior was the sin of the earlier ages, from the days of Cain; and non-submission to this promised Seed as King and Lord was the sin of succeeding times from Nimrod downward. The world's after-history in all lands, and empires, and religions, shows us these two united; and earth to this day holds on in her old course of non-subjection to her rightful King. Babylon, Assyria, and Egypt have their counterparts in the modern kingdoms of the world. Lords many, kings many, emperors many, usurpers many, earth has had, and to them it has bowed the knee. But to this one King of the Father's choosing, anointing, and enthroning, it will vow no allegiance; or gives at the most, mouth-honor, breath, which the poor heart would fain deny, but dare not. He that sitteth in the heavens doth laugh, but He has yet descended to speak to them in His wrath, nor to vex them in His sore displeasure. God is standing in the congregation of the mighty; He judgeth among the gods, saying, How long will ye judge unjustly, and accept the person of the wicked? But they know not, neither will they understand; and God has not yet risen to judge the earth, nor to depose its rebellious dynasties, nor to constrain the obedience of the nations, nor to bring to pass the promised service of loyal love from the sons of the first Adam to their true Head and Kinsman the 'second man,' the Lord from heaven. The revolt is as wide spread as ever, and it is only a handful, a remnant here and there, the result of God's eternal election, that owns Him as Head and Lord. The rest are blinded and hardened: 'Who is Lord over us?' is the cry of earth. All the world wonders after the beast, worships him, received his name in their forehead and in their hand. The spirit of antichrist is lawlessness, the contrast and contradiction of Him who magnified the law, and made to honor. Antichrist is the self-exalting one, the opposer of God and His Christ; his aim is the monarchy of earth. The personification of all rebellion and self-will, he does his utmost to perpetuate and extend the world's non-reception of Christ, to prevent all things being put under Him.

As King, Christ is Judge; but the world accepts not His judgment; it believes not in His acquittals and His condemnations, either now or hereafter. His sentences, as moral verdicts of approval or disapproval, they may receive; but as judicial decisions of the highest court of appeal, inferring irreversibly the recompense of a glorious heaven or an unquenchable hell, they repudiate them. In this sense Christ is not Judge, and there is no judgment day, and no great white throne. All things are not yet put under Him as Judge!

As King, He is Avenger, but the day of recompense had not yet come, and 'sentence against an evil work' has not yet been executed. Therefore, not only does the world reject Him as the Avenger, but a large section of modern Christianity disowns the very idea of vengeance, as incompatible with love;

and the effeminate theologies of the age refuse to believe that the wrath of the Lamb is a reality, that the day of vengeance is in His heart, or the rod of iron in His hand. They have yet to learn the divine antipathy to sin, and the divine determination either to pardon or to punish eternally every sin, and every fragment of a sin, on whomsoever it shall be found. They have yet to understand the meaning of these awful words, 'I will tread them in mine anger, and trample them in my fury.'

As King, He is the Conqueror, but though His great victory is won, His conquest is not yet complete. The routed host still rallies, disputes the field, nay, recovers ground so widely, that men ask, Where is the Conqueror, and where is His victory? Heathendom is as populous and as idolatrous as ever, and Christendom is yet more hostile to Christ and the Christianity than paganism of old. The sway of antichrist is vast; and Satan is not yet bound, but goes to and fro throughout the earth, the inspirer of its false religions, the instigator of its rebellion, the forger of its errors, the soul of antichrist, the spirit that now worketh in the children of disobedience.

As King, He is Deliverer, the opener of all prisons, and the looser of all chains. But the gates of brass are not yet broken, nor the bars of iron cut asunder. The curse still poisons the soil and troubles its tillers — the curse of barrenness, disease, pain, weariness, vanity, the sweating toil of man, and the travail pangs of woman. The wilderness has not yet been glad, nor the desert blossomed as the rose.

As King, He is the Resurrection and the Life; but the dead have not yet risen, the grave has not refunded its ill-gotten treasure. The dust of saints, though precious in His sight, is undistinguishable from the mold of earth; and forms beloved of Him and beloved of us are still prey of corruption. He has the keys of Hades and death, but He has not unlocked their two-leaved gates, nor said to the prisoners to go forth. The churchyards of earth have not yet been emptied, nor has the sea delivered up its dead. The worm still feeds on bodies which are parts of Christ's body, and the Head has not yet interposed. The shroud still wraps forms which are the temples of the Holy Ghost, and He who has the residue of the Spirit has not yet rescued one particle of that holy dust. Death still reigns, and 'he who has the power of death' still continues to slay. The tomb still holds the countless atoms of redeemed morality, and this corruptible has not yet put on incorruption. Death, the last enemy, has not yet been destroyed, and the grave can still boast of its victory.

Now we see not yet all things out under Him; but we see Jesus on the Father's throne, crowned with glory above, in anticipation of the like crown below. For earth's long rebellion shall come to a 'perpetual end.' Each spoiler shall be spoiled, each conqueror conquered, each prison opened, each boaster silenced, each blasphemer confounded, each anti-christ smitten, each rival throne overturned, when 'the Christ' shall take to Himself His great power and reign.

ENDNOTES

Chapter 1

[1] It may be well here to advert to the exact meaning of the word church. It is not the true translation of the scriptural word which originally signified an assembly of the citizens summoned by the crier (see Liddell and Scott), and is retained in the French *`eglise* and the Italian *chiesa*. The English word *church* is the same as the German *Kirche* and the Scottish *kirk*, which three words come from the Greek, and signify 'the Lord's House' or building, as an old Latin writer (about A.D. 840) tells us: 'abipsis autem Gracis Kyrch, a Kyrios, et alia multa accepimus; sicut domus Dei, Basilica, i.e. regia a Rege, sic etiam Kysica, i.e. Dominica a Domino nuncupatur' (See Trench, *On the Study of Words*, p. 68). Thus the word church signified properly the *building*, and not the *people*. Some have objected to our calling the *building* by the name *church*; but this is really the proper term, and it is our translators who have erred in giving 'church' instead of 'assembly' or 'congregation,' as the rendering of

all such passages as Eph. 5:25- 26, where Tysdale and Cranmer, following the Greek, give us 'Christ the head of the *congregation*,' and 'Christ loved the *congregation*.' From these two translators probably it was that the early Scotch Reformers used *congregation* for *church*, as in 'the Band subscribed by the Lords' in 1557: we read, 'the gospel of Christ and His *congregation*;' and again, 'the majesty of God and His *congregation*; 'and again, 'the most blessed word of God and his *congregation* – though afterwards they used the expression 'Christe's Kirke.' In modern times the term, 'the church', has acquired a sort of mystical meaning, and may be used as the synonym for some undefined spiritual personage or being; whereas this word 'church', to which so many superstitious ideas (both Popish and Protestant) have been attached, does not occur in Scripture at all, except as the English representation of an incorrect translation of the Greek. And were we to return to the more exact rendering of 'assembly,' or congregation,' or 'gathering,' many false ideas would be dispelled, and some true ones exchanged for them. Let us first go to the Old Testament, and there we shall find God's people called by the same Hebrew, Greek, and Latin words as have been rendered *church* by our translators in the New Testament. We can only take a few of these, but they are specimens of a large class (Num. 19:20), 'That soul shall be out off from among the congregation,' or CHURCH, if we accept the word by our translators in the New Testament. In the Vulgate ecclesia, in Junius and Tremellius congregation. Deut 18:16, 'according to all that thou desirest of the

Lord thy God in Horeb, in the day of the *assembly*' (or church). Deut, 23:1, 'shall not enter into the *congregation* of the Lord,' or 'into the *church* of the Lord:' 31:30, 'Moses spake in the ears of the *congregation* (church) of Israel the words of this song.' Josh. 8:35, 'Before all the congregation (church) of Israel.' Judg. 20:2, 'The chief of the people presented themselves in the assembly (church) of the people of God.' Judg. 21:5, 'Who is there that came not up with the *congregation* (church) unto the Lord?' 1 Sam 17:47, 'All this *assembly* (church) shall know that the Lord saveth not with sword and spear.' 1 Kings 8:14, The king blessed all the *congregation* (church) of Israel.' See also 1 Chron. 13:2, 4, 28:8, 29:1,10:20; 2 Chron. 1:3, 6:3, 20:15, 'The Spirit of the Lord in the midst of the *congregation*' (church), etc. But see especially Ps. 22:22 (quoted by the apostle in Heb. 2:12), 'In the midst of the *congregation* (church) will I praise Thee;' and ver. 25, 'My praise shall be of Thee in the great *congregation*' (church). Ps. 26:12, 'In the *congregation* (churches) will I bless the Lord.' Ps. 35:18, 'I will give Thee thanks in the great *church*.' Ps. 40:9, 'I have preached righteousness in the great *church*.' Ps 68:26 'Bless ye God in the *churches*.' Ps. 89:5, 'Thy faithfulness in the *churches* of the saints.' Ps. 149:1 'Sing unto the Lord a new song, and His praise in the *church* of His saints.' From these passages we see that the word *church* in its real sense is an Old Testament word, and that the apostle took this Greek name for it from the Old Testament; so that which we call 'the church,' but which the Holy Spirit calls the assembly or congregation, was found among the Old Testament saints; and that it was the 'church,' or congregation, or 'commonwealth of Israel' (Eph. 2:12), that the New Testament saints were added. Of this, 'the church in the wilderness,' as Stephan calls it (Acts 7:11), was part: it was to this Old Testament assembly that our Lord referred when He said, 'Tell it unto the *church*...if he neglect to hear the *church*' (Matt. 23:17); and His allusion to the 'heathen' (Gentiles) and 'publican' shows that He was referring to the *church* of Old Testament times: 'tell it to the *congregation*' is the rendering of Tyndale and Cranmer. It may be that 'the *church* of the firstborn', or as Tyndale renders it, 'the congregation of the firstborn sonnes' (Heb. 12:23), refers to the Old Testament saints to whom the New Testament ones had come and been made 'fellow-citizens with the saints' (of the Old Testament); nay, become 'of the *household* of God' (Eph. 2:19). Thus, what is called 'the church,' or the 'assembly,' or 'congregation,' is composed of all saints from the beginning' the New Testament saints being honored, to be the *fellow-citizens with the ancient saints* — relations of God, as Israel was ('Ephraim is my firstborn'), and sharers of the glory of patriarchs and prophets. All from the beginning were included in one purpose of election, washed in one blood, clothed with one righteousness, made members of one body ('My dead body shall then arise,' says Christ, speaking by Isaiah of Old Testament saints), stones in one living temple, filled by one Spirit, all eating the same spiritual meat and drinking the same drink, and heirs of one common glory in the Kingdom and city of the Lord, the New Jerusalem, of which they are made 'fellow-citizens' here.

CHAPTER 4

[1] The words literally run thus, 'The Coming One into the world;' for Messiah was known to Israel by this name, 'the Coming One.' Afterwards He is named 'the Come One' (1 John 4:3 v.6). Thus, 'He is come' contained the gospel, or good news, which an Israelite would well understand; The 'good things' connected with Him as 'the Christ' and as 'the High Priest' are similarly referred to: for He is said to be 'the High Priest of the good things to come' (Heb. 9:11); which good things are not exhausted by His first coming, which are yet to be poured out more abundantly at His second. This is 'the grace that is to be brought unto us at the revelation of Jesus Christ' (1 Pet. 1:13).

[2] I find that by some a mystical meaning is attached to the word 'abiding,' whereas it simply means 'remaining,' and ought always to have been translated by one word, either abiding or remaining. Others, I find, affirm that such expressions as Christ being *in* us, or the Spirit being *in* us, are peculiar to the New Testament, whereas they are quite common in the Old; and the Old Testament word 'among you' is that which is rendered 'in you' in the New Testament. The Old Testament saints had 'the indwelling Spirit' as truly as the

New. Indeed, all the New Testament expressions regarding the Spirit are taken from the Old. Ex. 29:45; Judg. 14:6; Isa. 63:11; Ezek. 2:2.

[3] The Greek rather gives a slightly different thought in connection with the above passage, and we might render the words thus: 'O fools, and slow of heart to believe, after all that the prophets have spoken.' To believe what? To believeth the *resurrection*, to which they had just referred. The Lord reproached them with their slow belief of the *resurrection*, notwithstanding all that the prophets have spoken.

CHAPTER 5

[1] In the proceeding prediction from Isaiah, we may notice the same expression as to the naming of the child. In the former it is, '*she shall call* His name Immanuel;' in the latter it is, '*thou shall call* His name Jesus.'

[2] Some in our day refuse to pray for the Spirit, and think it sinful to ask Him to come, seeing He has already come. On the same principle, they would have objected to those who, when Christ was here, asked Him to 'come' (see John 4:47, 49, 14:23). Christ had come, yet men asked Him to come; and He came! He came to them individually, or to their house. So the spirit has come; yet we ask Him to come; and He cometh! We ask Him to come into us, or to our friends, or to our city. We do not mean to deny that He came at Pentecost, but still we ask Him to come to us. When we ask for the

teaching, it is as if we said, O Spirit, come and teach us; come and enlighten us; come and quicken us. Does He teach without coming to us? Is He a mere *influence*, as men indicate when they speak of 'divine influences'? Does He not enter into the soul on conversion? Does he not come in, when as the Comforter, He comforts? Is He not our guest, dwelling in us, and working in us? Such quibbles about words are unworthy of Christians.

[3] Some in our day made use of a peculiar phraseology to express the believer's complete exemption from judgment. 'We stand beyond our doom,' they say. Not so. 'We must all appear before the judgment seat of Christ.' We might as well say that we stand beyond death, because we have been 'quickened together with Christ;' or beyond resurrection, because we have 'risen with Christ.' Let us beware of pushing Scripture figures too far. God has graciously written them down for us, to show us how complete our acquittal is, but let us not go beyond the words themselves. We are still on this side of resurrection and the judgment. The rest will follow in the due time.

[4] It is 'bruising,' not extinction, nor annihilation, far less restoration, that is predicted regarding the great adversary. What the eternal bruising of the serpent's head may fully mean, we cannot say. We must be content with such passages as the twentieth of Revelation, especially ver. 10, and Matt. 25:41.

CHAPTER 7

[1] The words 'creation' and 'workmanship' remind us of the expressions used in reference to the first creation, 'His work which God *created* and *made*' (Gen 2:3).

CHAPTER 9

[1] The expression which we have in the above verse is used more than once by the Apostle Paul in reference to the churches as a whole. He writes 'to the Church of the Thessalonians which is IN God the Father, and IN the Lord Jesus Christ' (1 Thess. 1:1; 2 Thess. 1:1) Thus, that which John applies to each individual saint is applied by Paul to the Church at large. In the special passage on which the remarks in this chapter are founded; it may be well to notice that, while in our translation there are *three* words used — 'abiding,' 'remaining,' and 'continuing' — there is only *one* in the Greek. This greatly misleads the common reader, making him think that there are three distinct states set forth. There ought to have been but *one* word in the translation, and it does not much matter which of the three English words is employed; only, as we find a sort of mystical halo thrown round the word, 'abiding,' it would be better to use 'remain' or 'continue.' Instead of 'remain' or 'continue,' we have many places where simply the words 'to be' are used. 'We are in the true One' (1 John 5:20). The same word is used of the anointing or

unction, in ver. 27, 'The anointing which ye have received of Him abideth (remaineth) in you;' and according to the 'remaining' of the 'anointing' is our remaining in Christ — 'As it hath taught you, ye shall abide in Him' (ver. 27).

CPSIA information can be obtained at www.ICGtesting.com
262878BV00001B/2/P

9 781613 790496